Surveying the flurry of crit
that *The Waste Land* inspi
Eliot commented, "I regret
 ⸱nꞯuirers off on a
         ⸱ᵈₛ and

philosophical, critical, and poetic work, and establishes Eliot's place in contemporary critical arguments. Davidson ultimately focuses on *The Waste Land*, using examples from that poem to display a hermeneutic view of world and self.

Davidson's reading centers on the qualities of absence and fragmentation in *The Waste Land*. Because there is no consistent narrative persona, or "controlling consciousness," in the poem, and no fixed structure of meaning, the reader's expectations of definition and limitation are frustrated. However, Davidson argues, this very fragmentation "releases meaning into the play of a human world rich with possibilities, even if destitute of certainties." In the absence of fixed meaning and in the face of a multiplicity of possibilities, there is for Davidson a hermeneutic ontology, a universe of connections, a cycle of perpetually deferred meaning. Her interpretation is radically new, and her arguments are provocative and persuasive.

T. S. Eliot and Hermeneutics

Harriet Davidson

T. S. Eliot
and Hermeneutics

Absence and Interpretation
in *The Waste Land*

Louisiana State University Press
Baton Rouge and London

1935 1985

Designer: Joanna Hill
Typeface: Linotron Trump and Eras
Typesetter: Moran Colorgraphic
Printer and binder: Edwards Brothers

Publication of this book has been assisted by a grant from the Andrew W. Mellon Foundation.

Library of Congress Cataloging in Publication Data

Davidson, Harriet.
   T. S. Eliot and hermeneutics.

   Bibliography: p.
   Includes index.
   1. Eliot, T. S. (Thomas Sterns), 1888–1965. Waste land. I. Title.
PS3509.L43W3642   1985   821'.912   84-21757
ISBN 0-8071-1208-9

Grateful acknowledgment is made to Faber and Faber Ltd. for permission to quote from these works by T. S. Eliot: *Collected Poems 1909–1962, Knowledge and Experience in the Philosophy of F. H. Bradley, Selected Essays, On Poetry and Poets, After Strange Gods,* "Isolated Superiority," from *The Dial,* 84 (1928), and "London Letter," from *The Dial,* 70 (1921). Quotations from *The Sacred Wood: Essays on Poetry and Criticism* are used by permission of Methuen, Inc. Excerpts from *Knowledge and Experience in the Philosophy of F. H. Bradley,* copyright © 1964 by T. S. Eliot, are reprinted by permission of Farrar, Straus and Giroux, Inc.

■ For Bruce

1485

B4T

11-18-05

Contents

Acknowledgments

This book would never have been written without the inspiration and guidance of Vereen Bell, who has always encouraged me, in his own way. I wish to thank Donald Ault for his many helpful suggestions on this manuscript and Roy Gottfried and T. D. Young for the time and support they gave me. I am also indebted to the memorable classes of Charles Scott, where I learned Heidegger, and Dudley Andrew, where I was introduced to the writings of Paul Ricoeur. Finally, I am grateful to J. Hillis Miller for the insightful and sympathetic reading he gave this manuscript.

Any statement would be inadequate to acknowledge how much this book is dependent on the philosophical understanding, poetic insight, and psychological support of my husband Bruce Tucker.

Even these lived truths are partial and fragmentary, for the finest tact after all can give us only an interpretation, and every interpretation, along with perhaps some utterly contradictory interpretation, has to be taken up and reinterpreted by every thinking mind and every civilization.

T. S. Eliot
Knowledge and Experience
in the Philosophy of F. H. Bradley

T. S. Eliot and Hermeneutics

Absence and Density
in *The Waste Land*

Even this doom of the gods remaining absent is a way in which the world worlds.

Martin Heidegger
"The Origin of the Work of Art"

I

The title *The Waste Land* has a wealth of possible references: it is the mythical land deprived of fertility by its ruler's weakness; it invokes the legendary England of the Arthurian quest; it evokes a war-stricken Europe; and it may represent the spiritual state of modern civilization. In each case "Waste" suggests a state of depletion, barrenness, and emptiness—"*Oed' und leer das Meer.*" But "to waste" can also designate an action that subtly suggests the opposite of its adjectival form. And this poem is wasteful in exactly this sense of excess, of plenitude beyond consumption. *The Waste Land* suggests too much, so that any attempt to define a meaning for the poem must necessarily waste multiple other meanings. The poem, like its title, opens itself to a variety of symbolic and allusive references.

But the real sense of excess here is in the diacritical system of the poem whereby meaning is determined not by reference, but by the relation between elements in a system. *The Waste Land* is conspicuously lacking in the features of language that limit and define systemic meaning; instead it is complexly paratactic, connotative, and allusive. Again, the title is exemplary. A barren place is a wasteland. The stricken land of legend, following Jessie Weston, is "the Land Laid Waste" or "the Waste Land."[1] The definite article raises a common wasteland to a significant, perhaps symbolic one. And, diacritically, the separation of "Waste" from "Land" gives possibility to the noun form of "waste," which must be defined in some degree of opposition to "land." The gap between "waste" and "land" maintains a fine distinction between a barren waste and a fertile land, as if in that blank space, that absence, were guarded the possibility for renewal without which The Waste Land could have no symbolic purpose.

The poem gives these diacritical possibilities maximum play by consistently foregrounding such gaps. It is a poem full of strategic absences. Thematically, the poem gives us the absence of love, of life, of belief, and to some extent, of meaning. Formally, the absences are as interesting and as striking. The controlling rhetorical figure in the poem is allusion, a device which, I will argue, signifies in deference to certain kinds of absences. The grammar of the poem is heavily paratactic; logical and syntactical connections are often absent. The larger structure of the poem is also paratactic in its seemingly unrelated series of fragmented narratives and lyrics, connected only by allusive section titles and themes. Sometimes from word to word, often from line to line, and virtually always from episode to episode, our first experience as readers of The Waste Land is of the absence of expected connections or sources. Our second experience, if experience could be so cataloged, would surely be of the density of possibilities corresponding to these absences.

But the most important absence in the poem, the absence which underlies the formal and thematic absences, is the absence of a persona. This is a vexed issue in The Waste Land, and much energy has gone into finding the missing consciousness of the poem. Still,

---

1. Jessie Weston, *From Ritual to Romance* (1920; rpr. Garden City, N. Y., 1957), 18 *passim*.

the many voices of the poem cannot be reconciled into anything we know of as a single self, while the extremely personal and unique sense of the poem belies the notion of some universal consciousness or collective unconscious. The poem simply does not have what we would identify as a controlling consciousness, and this absence is a powerful and disturbing one.

Absence is the primary communication of the poem, communicating, to paraphrase Eliot, before it is understood. Many of our best critics have pointed out that this poem can be meaningful to even the uninformed reader who does not know the Grail legend, or recognize the allusions, or have any of the secondary knowledge which we bring to the poem in seeking understanding.[2] Although the semantic content of the poem does communicate themes of loss and lack, absence is also communicated in two other, more primary ways. First, the poem makes the reader experience the absence of expected connections. This reader-response observation capitalizes on the existential confusion which readers may feel and does not necessarily lead us beyond the state of subject confronting object. Secondly, and more profoundly, the poem discloses absence ontologically as a state of the world, not as the state of a consciousness trying to know a world. This second, crucial definition will be taken up at length in Chapter Two with an examination of the philosophy of Martin Heidegger in which absence (as always concealed Being) is a central dynamic force setting in motion a world which is interpretive—or, hermeneutic—in its very nature.

The terms *absence* and *hermeneutic* are central for my argument and will take some extensive discussion to define. For now, let me specify that by *absence* I mean the absence of a transcendent foundation, center, origin—whether subjective or objective—for our being. Because of this absence of transcendence, interpretation or *hermeneutics*, rather than empirical certainty or innate ideas, becomes the foundation for meaning in the world. This post-Heideg-

2. Hugh Kenner and Ezra Pound are the major critics insisting that the poem is meaningful without knowledge of the secondary material. See below, section III.

gerian hermeneutics is the process of creating meaning in the absence of any ultimate foundation for truth, a process revealed, in part, in the diacritical function of language. The technique of *The Waste Land* discloses this ontological absence and this process of interpretation. The poem resists any attempt to encompass it by a coherent psychological, structural, or logical idea; the poem's existence, like the voice of the woman in the pub in "A Game of Chess," is real, meaningful and defiantly untranslatable. The poem reveals a world which is almost totally concealed from us in our desire for structures to explain it, but is also meaningful in itself. What Heidegger calls concealedness is the most powerful form of absence in the poem and the one which ties together linguistic and thematic absences.

Curiously, in experiencing this absence in *The Waste Land*, we are not experiencing the desolation of a wasteland. That theme of emptiness has been taken up by existentialists such as Camus, Sartre, and often Hemingway, who so powerfully manipulate language toward a minimum of referential and diacritical possibility and thus retain the dominance of the existential I AM over a meaningless and indifferent world. But no one has ever confused these landscapes with that of *The Waste Land*. Rather, Eliot's poem confronts us with a bewildering multiplicity caused not only by the fragmentation of the coherent world, but also by a fragmentation of the self. This fragmentation does not result in despair or emptiness or in the egocentric accrual of all meaning to the self as some existentialists have done. Rather, the fragmentation releases meaning into the play of a human world rich with possibilities, even if destitute of certainties. It is a peculiarly contemporary situation. In *The Waste Land* the disappearance of God is compounded by a disappearance of the self as an autonomous and unified whole, and the result is a poem radically new for its time and still not wholly assimilated today.

The poem's persistent lack of clear signification opens up the possibility of a metaphoric connection at every turn, leading to a multiplicity of interpretations. The brilliance of Eliot's formal ex-

periments is that no amount of subsequent reading will totally remove the absences in the poem. The opacity remains stubbornly
there, not dissolved by any interpretation. Instead, the poem seems
to expose the conditions for the possibility of all interpretations of
this text and any text. Prior to the essentialist's assertion of meaning, or to the existentialist's recognition of meaninglessness, is
man's state within the world (being-in-the-world, if you will) which
necessarily precedes these judgments.

The existentialists may make up for a lack of external authority
with the controlling consciousness. Without either, the world
changes entirely. We are left with a rather indiscriminate, though
not necessarily meaningless, jumble of events, characters, thoughts,
texts, memories, and desires out of which the self must be created
and create. This state holds much fascination for Eliot, not only for
the delicious oppression it offers the romantic Prufrockian consciousness, but also for the poetic and ontological possibilities it
offers the anti-romantic consciousness of Eliot. Eliot had a lifelong
intuition, most strongly stated in "Tradition and the Individual
Talent," that poetry was dissociated from the poet. His most com-
monly known poetic dicta reveal his suspicion that the ego is not
the source of creativity. For Eliot, poems communicate apart from
rational understanding; the power of expression is carried by the
"external facts," the objective correlative, not internal states; the
poet's mind is only the catalyst—the shred of platinum which sets
off a reaction it does not enter into. The substance of the poem is
not interior any more than it is empirical; rather it is a gathering up
of the tradition in a particular moment. The only authority rests in
the unstable hands of culture, and culture is uniquely both subjective and objective in that it is created yet it creates, both temporal
and timeless in that it retains everything in a state of continual
change, both personal and universal in that it is both homogeneous
and a unique horizon from every point within it. In short, the self
becomes a locus of culture with no transcendental dominion over
the cultural matrix.

Now, the autonomous self is one of our most cherished ideas, a strong legacy of romanticism with which the artist, in particular, is often unwilling to part. But for Eliot, the idea of the self was always problematic. In the early poetry Eliot portrays a sense of solipsistic relativity and stifling subjectivity, but his use of clear personae and his ironic stance reveal his ambivalence about the difference between the artist who creates and communicates and the trapped souls of Prufrock and Sweeney. Through philosophy, Eliot found a first solution to this problem in a critique of subject/object dualism. Particularly in his work on F. H. Bradley and in "Tradition and the Individual Talent," Eliot examines the mystique of the self and finds, at least at the point of *The Waste Land*, that relativity does not necessarily imply subjectivity. This is an extremely difficult position to hold, as many of our contemporary philosophers show us, and only recently has this belief become widespread. Eliot soon abandoned this position for a second solution, religion, but even here, or especially here, the self is at fault, now before God.

Eliot's distrust of the self is a critical commonplace, illumined most frequently by reference to the self-abnegation of the religious poetry, to the insecurity of the Prufrock period poems, or to Eliot's prose indictments of the cult of personality. But the least coherent statements about Eliot's attitude toward the self have been made in regard to *The Waste Land*, the poem in which Eliot's critique of the self is most central, most radical, and most complex. The critical problem has been, I believe, a methodological one. Early, but still major critics such as Cleanth Brooks, F. R. Leavis, and Joseph Frank, have approached *The Waste Land* structurally, looking for underlying mythic, symbolic, or formal coherence. But these structural, New Critical approaches, while often helpful, do not and cannot adequately encompass the problematic of the self. A structure is an epistemological heuristic—a way of knowing which cannot help us when the ontology of the knower is at issue. Most structural approaches, which still today dominate study of *The Waste Land*, assume the presence of *a priori* rational structures in a controlling consciousness of the poem or the reader, and then move on to epistemological concerns; or, as William Spanos has pointed out in a recent article on the poem, they end up treating the structures as essences.[3]

Because critics have not been able to confront a central aspect of the text—the absence of a persona—they have not been able to explain adequately the meaning of *The Waste Land* in a way that accounts for the distinctive texture of the poem. The repeated claims that the poem depicts modern fragmentation in the face of encroaching technology, that the poem compares a mythic past to a deracinated present, or that the poem recovers meaning for the modern world could be made about many late nineteenth century poems, while the immediate impression of Eliot's poem is that, formally at least, it marks a radical break with the past. In *The Waste Land* Eliot's formal divergence from tradition is part of a coherent intellectual divergence from traditional ways of thinking about the world. The poem, along with some of Eliot's prose statements of the same period, represents a new and radical being-in-the-world, one that breaks completely with the agonized epistemological concerns of his dualist predecessors. The loss of the self combined with the loss of God mourned by earlier poets results in a world which is non-romantic, non-existential, and non-psychological. Instead, we now have what, since Heidegger, has been called the linguistic universe,[4] but, to avoid the suggestion of radical nominalism, I would like to call it the *hermeneutic* universe, a term I will explain in full in Chapter Two.

Critical theory has only recently absorbed the implications of a linguistic world which denies the romantic self, so that now we are in a position to interpret *The Waste Land* somewhat differently than has been done in the past by establishing a critical context in which a radical critique of the self is possible and absence and interpretation are central. This task will lean heavily upon the linguis-

3. William Spanos, "Repetition in *The Waste Land*: A Phenomenological Destruction," *Boundary 2*, VII (Spring, 1979), 225–85.

4. Heidegger's work after his reversal focuses increasingly on language as foundational. Whereas in Chapter Two I will try to ground my discussion of Heidegger in the structures of *Being and Time*, for this essay Heidegger's later work on language and art is most inspirational.

tic turn in twentieth-century philosphy for documentation, but the initial questions about absence, meaning, and the self remain rooted in the poem. The circularity of a hermeneutic is evident here. By taking absence seriously in *The Waste Land*, we must experience a shift, or indeed a revolution, in all of our assumptions about language and the world; the world reinterprets itself around a new insight. But the initial questions about the poem could never have been asked without using language in which these new assumptions are already inherent. So that a new interpretation involves an enormous, but involuntary, change, difficult to trace in rational discourse. Insight comes in a flash, we say, as a whole, with the particular and universal defining each other, a message from the unpredictable Hermes himself.

II

In order to highlight the common assumptions which have dominated previous criticism of *The Waste Land* and have led readers away from various elements in the poem, I will spend the third section of this chapter examining major trends in criticism of this poem. That discussion will lay the groundwork for the theoretical work in Chapter Two, which will document the hermeneutic universe demanded by the poem by using the authority of two major trends in twentieth-century thought. First, I will describe briefly the theory of language advanced by Ferdinand de Saussure, which involves a necessary decentering of the self from creation of meaning. Although Saussure is generally connected with structuralist thought and the canonization of *langue* over *parole*, my own interest in Saussure is in the implications of the arbitrary and diacritical constitution of the sign for living discourse. Next, I will attempt to summarize the complex philosophy of Heidegger which demystifies the subject in his analysis of Being-in-the-world. Although Heidegger is my philosophical touchstone, the history of the demystification of consciousness includes the diversity of Freud, Marx, and Nietzsche and has produced contemporary thinkers as different as Jacques Derrida and Paul Ricoeur. For these philosophers, human subjectivity is no longer the center of meaning (nor is God), no longer existent in the usual romantic sense. In fact, such thinkers reject subject/object dualism in favor of an understanding of human being as created by the world.

Increasingly, demystifying philosophers have turned their attention to the place where self and world are most indistinguishable—language, an entity intimately personal yet radically other, individually creative yet culturally determined. For Eliot, I am most interested in the manifestation of linguistic demystification in the Heideggerian hermeneutics defined by Hans-Georg Gadamer and Paul Ricoeur, rather than in Derridian semiotics. Though both philosophies share the notion of a finite, linguistic universe, hermeneutics is interested in the truth of art and the generative and transforming power of language, which is lacking in deconstructive semiotics. Contemporary hermeneutics restructures traditional theories of meaning, of aesthetics, of history, and of the self in a way that concurs remarkably with some of Eliot's early statements about poetry and clarifies the nature of his most difficult early poetry.

Chapters Three and Four will review Eliot's prose writings that contribute to a critique of consciousness. His dissertation on Bradley is of great interest here, for while much work has been done on the dissertation recently, particularly as a gloss on Eliot's criticism and later poetry, very little thought has been given to the connection between *The Waste Land* and Bradley, even though Bradley's influence on Eliot was strongest during these years. In light of recent developments in criticism, Bradley's skepticism, rejection of dualism, and ideas about the self emerge as serious influences on Eliot's art. Of course, "Tradition and the Individual Talent" is also a touchstone here. This richest of all of Eliot's essays is clearly influenced by the dissertation written three years before and is often taken as a gloss on *The Waste Land* written two years later. Eliot's famed impersonal theory of poetry has yet to be given its due as a critique of subject/object dualism which so occupied Bradley. Less striking, but important are Eliot's early essays for the *Criterion* in which he blasts Romanticism and the cult of the individual. These early essays, as John Margolis has thoroughly documented, show Eliot's consistent disdain for the autonomy and effectiveness of the individual, an attitude that eventually led him toward the acceptance of external authority in the form of church and state.[5]

Finally, the last chapter will focus on *The Waste Land*. This major section will cover a number of issues related to the absence of the self from the world and the implications of this absence for poetic form. The method of my discussion of the poem involves a circular hermeneutic. Beginning from the common perception that loss is central to the poem I was simultaneously led more deeply into the poem to a discovery of absence in the formal elements such as allusion, metonymy, and narrative, and away from the poem to more general modes of thought, such as hermeneutic theory and contemporary psychoanalysis, which find the absence of essences to be central to human being. These two movements of criticism are mutually dependent to a large extent. The philosophy provides a language of meaningful interpretation for elements in the poem that have never been dealt with adequately, and the poem opens up a practical home for this difficult thought.

At this point I can only suggest some of the results of this study, but perhaps these suggestions will clarify some subsequent material. The difficulties of the poem stem from the merging of the poet with his landscape; there is no controlling voice of consciousness in the poem. Instead, many voices, fragments of literature, songs, paintings, prophets, even the thunder, speak to us. Through these many voices, the poem discloses a world that speaks to us, a world where everything is given to us already linguistically, thus humanly, interpreted. This intimate participation between man and world disallows any transcendent subjectivity or objectivity. The peculiar quality of human life has not to do with absolute knowledge, but with the ontological absence of absolute knowledge caused by the finitude of our existence. This absence leads to the necessity of an open and interpretive being. The achievement of *The Waste*

5. John D. Margolis, *T. S. Eliot's Intellectual Development, 1922–1939* (Chicago, 1972).

Land is that it faces this finitude in both form and content and finds the uniquely human value of our least valued quality.

III

The Waste Land has always offered critics particularly difficult problems for the interpretation of meaning. From the time of its publication in 1922, there have been critics willing to declare it a failure, totally lacking in meaningful signification, while other critics will grant it emotive meaning but not ideational meaning (and vice versa, as in Hart Crane's remark, "It was good, of course, but so damned dead"[6]). Even the supporters of the poem are in broad disagreement about what the poem means and how it means. It is widely held to be a poem of despair and disillusionment, though there are those who see in it the way to faith and salvation. And those critics who wisely choose to discuss technique in lieu of theme still debate the working of the poem's structure and "mythical method."

This conflict of interpretations is inevitable in a poem so rich with enigma, enigma which, as Paul Ricoeur tells us, "does not block understanding, but provokes it."[7] Ricoeur's work in hermeneutics or interpretation theory, growing out of the tradition of Dilthey and Heidegger, can be of help with a poem which is provocative to a fault in some critics' minds. The great lesson we have learned from modern hermeneutics is that the questions we ask determine the answers we find, and the historical moment we inhabit determines the questions we ask. This statement will be taken up again in Chapter Two; for now let it serve as a means to gain an overview of the kinds of questions which have been asked about *The Waste Land*.

6. Quoted in Jay Martin, "T. S. Eliot's *The Waste Land*," in Jay Martin (ed.), *A Collection of Critical Essays on "The Waste Land"* (Englewood Cliffs, N.J., 1968), 6.
7. Paul Ricoeur, *Freud and Philosophy: An Essay on Interpretation*, trans. Denis Savage (New Haven, 1970), 18.

Ricoeur has bisected the range of interpretations into what he has called a "hermeneutics of suspicion" and a "hermeneutics of recovery,"[8] terms which correspond roughly to structuralism and phenomenology, respectively. But Ricoeur's use of the word *hermeneutics* in each term indicates his desire to avoid a duality in the ultimate goal of interpretation, even though the duality in method must be defined.

In a hermeneutics of suspicion the object—here, the poem—is suspect; its presence is an illusion to be dispelled. This hermeneutic strives for a displacement of meaning from the poem to underlying structures which may or may not be inferable from the poem itself. The clearest example of this type of interpretation is Freudian psychoanalysis, which most literally takes meaning out of the manifest consciousness and puts it into the latent unconscious where forces unknown, but inescapable, create meaning. This suspicion of consciousness is shared by two other great demystifiers, Marx and Nietzsche, who replace the primacy of conscious free will with the unseen workings of economic necessity and the will to power respectively.

Suspicion of a poem involves finding underlying structures which control meaning but are not immediately apparent in the act of reading. The greatest Anglo-American structuralist, Northrop Frye, puts himself squarely in the camp of suspicion when he says, "It is part of the critic's business to show how all literary genres are derived from the quest-myth."[9] Frye's work is perhaps representative of both the explanatory power and the reductive tendency of a hermeneutics of suspicion. The machine made of words becomes an assembly-line product, sacrificing the unique for the intricate.

Beginning with the publication of Eliot's own notes to *The Waste Land*, the hermeneutics of suspicion has dominated the interpretation of the poem. As Hugh Kenner has vigorously argued, these notes are in no way essential for the poem; but they remain structurally teasing.[10] Critics have been drawn to structural discussions

8. *Ibid.*, 27–36.
9. Northrop Frye, *Fables of Identity: Studies in Poetic Mythology* (New York, 1963), 17.
10. Hugh Kenner, *The Invisible Poet: T. S. Eliot* (New York, 1959), 150.

of this poem, partly because of its surface complexity, but also because of the difficulty, perhaps the impossibility, of talking meaningfully from the perspective of a dualist, romantic epistemology about a poem that lacks a persona.

The easiest way to solve the problem of meaning in the poem is to find that there is indeed a central persona.[11] This persona is generally taken to be Tiresias, following Eliot's note to the poem that "what Tiresias *sees* is the substance of the poem." Since Tiresias makes a rather brief appearance in the poem, it takes a great amount of suspicion to find his presence throughout. Of course, the appeal of Tiresias is that as immortal woman/man his consciousness would be totally unlike anything we could know; therefore the opacity of the poem can be "explained" in a wonderful critical evasion as the product of an inaccessible consciousness. Graham Hough insists that Tiresias functions as "not a single human consciousness, but a mythological catch-all, and as a unifying factor of no effect whatever."[12]

If not Tiresias, then some other quester is presumed to be the protagonist of the poem. Even those critics most willing to accept the fragmentary nature of the poem are driven at last to find a vague consciousness or personality uniting the fragments. Definitions of this personality range from being Eliot himself to a collective consciousness *à la* Jung,[13] but in no case is a unity of consciousness demonstrated in the poem. Critics suspect the fragmentary impact of the poem in favor of a general assumption of unity.

11. Grover Smith confidently assumes that Tiresias speaks the opening lines; see *T. S. Eliot's Poetry and Plays: A Study in Sources and Meaning* (Chicago, 1956), 72–76. See also Gertrude Patterson, *T. S. Eliot: Poems in the Making* (Manchester, 1971), 134; George Williamson, *A Reader's Guide to T. S. Eliot* (New York, 1953), 142; and Elizabeth Drew, *T. S. Eliot: The Design of His Poetry* (New York, 1949), 67.

12. Graham Hough, *Image and Experience* (London, 1960), 25.

13. J. Hillis Miller, *Poets of Reality* (New York, 1974), 172, and Drew, *Design*, 67, both speak of a collective consciousness in the poem. Kristian Smidt in *Poetry and Belief* (1949; rpr. London, 1961), 149, explicitly names the consciousness as Eliot's. Bernard Bergonzi in *T. S. Eliot* (New York, 1972), 99, calls the unifying voice an "ego rhythm." F. R. Leavis calls it "an inclusive human consciousness," in *New Bearings in English Poetry* (1932; rpr. Ann Arbor, 1960), 95. Critics such as Pound and Conrad Aiken imply some emotional unit which does not necessarily require a sense of consciousness (see below).

The many interpretations of *The Waste Land* based on the quest myth are perhaps most responsible for this desire for a quester. But more importantly, these interpretations must emphasize certain sections of the poem to the detriment of others in order to find the myth operating at all. The poem's final section most coherently uses the symbols of the myth, but curiously, this section is one of the least discussed parts of the poem. On the other hand, the relatively short Madame Sosostris episode has received disproportionate attention, because of its literal mention of the figures of the quest myth. This episode and its ironic tone have become the key to the mythical method of the poem. Major critics such as Cleanth Brooks, Helen Gardner, and Grover Smith have made the mythic interpretation a dominant one by tying myth to technique.[14]

Trying to preserve the density of the poem, Brooks describes the technique carefully:

> The basic method used in *The Waste Land* may be described as the application of the principle of complexity. The poet works in terms of surface parallelisms which in reality make ironical contrasts, and in terms of surface contrasts which in reality constitute parallelisms. . . . The two aspects taken together give the effect of chaotic experience ordered into a new whole, though the realistic surface of experience is faithfully retained. The complexity of the experience is not violated by the apparent forcing upon it of a predetermined scheme.[15]

Brooks's repetition of "in reality" as opposed to "surface" reveals what predetermined scheme *is* being forced upon the poem: the idea of ironic juxtaposition itself. I would not deny that certain kinds of irony do operate in *The Waste Land*, but the hegemony of mythic irony in discussions of Eliot's technique is still pervasive enough to

---

14. Cleanth Brooks, "*The Waste Land*: Critique of the Myth," *Modern Poetry and the Tradition* (Chapel Hill, N.C., 1939), rpr. in Martin (ed.), *A Collection of Critical Essays*, 59–86. Also, Helen Gardner, *The Art of T. S. Eliot* (London, 1949).

15. Brooks, "Critique of the Myth," 83.

warrant some critical refutation. Brooks takes the Madame Sosostris episode as his example, contrasting this scene with "the original use of the Tarot cards," but then refinding this "original" significance in the poem's further development as some episodes
connect to the mentioned Tarot. No doubt the repetitions and associations are important, but do they imply irony? That is, is there
indeed a summoning of an original, and I would assume, more dig-
nified use of the Tarot? Not within the poem, nor from the point of
view of a consistent satirical voice which would imply the missing
term. Brooks assumes a nostalgia for wholeness that does not exist
in the poem, where even the evocations of the past are as full of sadness, loss, death, and unfulfillment as the present events of the
poem.

I would suggest that the meaning of the segments of the poem is
defined neither by a supposed contrast nor a comparison with a
nostalgic, meaningful past, which could only exist in the mind of a
persona and be revealed in a consistent point of view or rhetorical
style. Brooks's interpretation implies that the events of the poem
could neither be properly degrading nor properly uplifting without
a central reference to a mythic structure. The presence of such a
central structure is always necessary for a method of ironic juxtaposition. The use of irony is derided as a "poetics of presence" by
certain contemporary philosophers.[16] That ironic centrality is just
what is most obviously absent in *The Waste Land*. How the poem
might be meaningful without a mythic center is clearly a question
that Brooks does not ask.

Another influential attempt to find meaning in *The Waste Land*
through technique is Joseph Frank's brilliant article on spatial form.
Frank's central insight reveals both his perception of the complexity of a poem like *The Waste Land* and his inability to find a vo-
cabulary or theory to account for this complexity:

> The meaning-relationship is completed by the simultaneous
> perception in space of word-groups which, when read con-

16. Spanos, "Repetition in *The Waste Land*," 229, discusses the Derridian
critique of irony.

secutively in time, have no comprehensible relation to each other. Instead of the instinctive and immediate reference of words and word-groups to the objects or events they symbolize, and the construction of meaning from the sequence of these references, modern poetry asks its readers to suspend the process of individual reference temporarily until the entire pattern of internal references can be apprehended as a unity.[17]

Like Brooks, Frank is unsure about how a "spatial" poem, which undermines causal sequence, might be meaningful. Evidently, a poem which proceeds logically would offer no problems for interpretation since it simply represents the empirical, objective world. But once one loses causality, Frank would have one move out of time and into idealism. Later in his essay, Frank explains that the pattern of analogous relationships in modern literature reveals "eternal prototypes" that "are created by transmuting the time world of history into the timeless world of myth."[18] Frank has two problems here. First, he is confusing causality with time, inferring from the lack of logical connection between episodes that the poem does not present a temporal world. William Spanos argues in his discussion of repetition in the poem that the very imposition of causality on experience falsifies the temporal world. Second, Frank is trapped in a romantic epistemology which sees the only alternative to the empirical world of history as the subjective world of myth or art. Since the particulars of the poem have "no comprehensible relation to each other," he puts them into suspicion in favor of a structure of myth. Frank is correct to see that a reference theory of meaning is inadequate for a poem like *The Waste Land*. But his solution is to replace reference to empirical objects with reference to a pattern of symbolic objects. And as always in a reference theory of meaning, these references are fixed and unproblematical, since meaning flows from the stable object to the word.

17. Joseph Frank, "Spatial Form in Modern Literature," *Sewanee Review*, LIII (1945), 229–30.
18. *Ibid.*, 229–30, 653.

Frank's attempt to describe technique is weakened by his need for a center—a still point. *The Waste Land* surely does impede forward movement by the reader because of the lack of syntactical connections and does require a type of spatial or metaphorical apprehension of connection rather than a metonymic understanding. But the critic's urge is to infer from this perception that the poem can be reduced to a single prototype, as Frank and Brooks do, or a single moment, as A. Walton Litz does when he asserts that *The Waste Land* is "an extended work that could be grasped by the mind as a single Image."[19] These major critics, who have dominated most subsequent thought about the poem, are, in virtue of their own metaphysics, unable to ask how, deprived of reason, essence, myth, we might still have meaning.

Another hermeneutic of suspicion attempts to explain the technique of *The Waste Land* in reference to other works of art, producing not altogether futile, but finally unsatisfying interpretations. Comparisons of this poem to music have not ever worked well, perhaps because critics have tried to use rational eighteenth-century musical forms for comparison, when twentieth-century jazz would probably be the most fruitful comparison. Jazz, like *The Waste Land*, employs both popular and classical idioms; traditional jazz experiments with rhythm while not straying far from a basic 4/4 beat, just as *The Waste Land* is grounded in iambic pentameter in spite of its seeming irregularity; and the emotional range of jazz is perhaps comparable to that of the poem. But, finally, music does not have the semantic/semiotic structure of language which is operating in this poem.

Comparisons to film and to Cubist art again are of limited value, perhaps more limited than musical comparisons, although much more frequent.[20] The "ineluctable modality of the visible" leads

19. A. Walton Litz, "*The Waste Land* Fifty Years After," in A. Walton Litz (ed.), *Eliot in His Time: Essays on the Occasion of the Fiftieth Anniversary of "The Waste Land"* (Princeton, 1973), 18.
20. See Jacob Korg, "Modern Art Techniques in *The Waste Land*," *Journal of Aesthetics and Art Criticism*, XVIII (1960), 456–63. For film comparisons see Lawrence Durrell, *A Key to Modern Poetry* (London, 1952), 143–44, and Anne Bolgan, *What the Thunder Really Said* (Montreal, 1973), 55–72.

Aristotle (and, more recently, Gadamer) to give language to hearing, not to sight. The substantiality of the visual arts in both form and content contrasts sharply with the abstract oddity of language. The allusive, metaphoric transformations of a poem like *The Waste Land* are in no way similar to montage, which may put things side by side but cannot change the nature—the entelechy—of the thing as metaphoric language can.

Recent critics of *The Waste Land* remain dominated by this tradition of a hermeneutics of suspicion. Anne Bolgan's *What the Thunder Really Said* is an admirable attempt to see the poem freshly by using Eliot's dissertation on Bradley to establish an intellectual context for the poem.[21] Unfortunately, the critic detours through Eisenstein's film theory for her major terms and ends up by finding the poem a failure in those terms. This is a hermeneutics of suspicion with a vengeance. A more straightforward attempt to describe the technique of this poem, M. Thormählen's exhaustive catalog *"The Waste Land": A Fragmentary Wholeness*, weakens its phenomenological usefulness with a familiar assumption: "As I see it, [*The Waste Land*] depicts a land inhabited by a race whose existence—characterized by aimless movement, daydreams and nightmares, failing communication, physical automatism, and a lurking uneasiness about to grow into terror—contrasts with *and* derives from past ages when a sense of direction was felt, even if the direction itself was a vicious one."[22] It is no wonder that this dominant trend in criticism of *The Waste Land* has led critics to approach the poem less and less as a meaningful whole and more and more as many isolated fragments to be analyzed and cataloged as shards of some yet to be discovered culture.

Ricoeur characterizes the opposite pole of interpretation as the restoration of meaning—a hermeneutics of recovery. Ricoeur's real interest, motivated by theological concerns, lies at this pole of interpretation, and this is where his thought is most original and

---

21. Bolgan, *What the Thunder Really Said*, 105–51.
22. Marianne Thormählen, *"The Waste Land": A Fragmentary Wholeness* (Lund, 1978), 216.

difficult. This hermeneutics proceeds not by suspicion, but by faith in the object. The hermeneutics of recovery has a "phenomenological care" for the object which wishes to describe it accurately without reducing it either to simply literal, univocal meaning or to abstract underlying structures. But there is a very real sense, especially with linguistic objects, that one cannot describe an object without first somehow knowing it; this knowledge Ricoeur calls a faith. This faith is not a simple faith, but a "post critical" faith: "It is a rational faith, for it interprets; but it is a faith because it seeks, through interpretation, a second naïvité. Phenomenology is its instrument of hearing, of recollection, of restoration of meaning. 'Believe in order to understand, understand in order to believe'—such is its maxim; and its maxim is the 'hermeneutic circle' itself of believing and understanding."[23]

The great phenomenologist Gaston Bachelard sums up this same paradox in his urging that imagination precedes perception.[24] In a literal sense, one does not see something that has no meaning in one's imagined world. And Eliot states his own version in his 1929 essay on Dante: "genuine poetry can communicate before it is understood."[25] Interpretation is understanding that initial communication which is addressed by the poem. For the hermeneutics of suspicion, initial belief or communication does not, theoretically, have to exist. The structuralist does not have to believe in the poem to interpret it; even detractors of *The Waste Land* have offered helpful structural interpretations of the poem. The phenomenologist must believe, that is have an initial engagement, an immediate sense of meaningfulness. This important point will be central later.

Attempts at the hermeneutics of recovery have been, historically, the most common form of interpretation. In its most degraded form, recovery is a *belles-lettres* approach to the "beauties" of a poem. But in the hands of a very great reader of literature this

23. Ricoeur, *Freud and Philosophy*, 28.
24. See Colette Gaudin (ed.), *On Poetic Imagination and Reverie: Selections from the Works of Gaston Bachelard* (New York, 1971), 10.
25. T. S. Eliot, *Selected Essays* (Rev. ed.; New York, 1950), 200.

approach gives us our most penetrating insights into art. When Coleridge begins his lecture on *Hamlet*, the first question he asks is profoundly phenomenological: "What did Shakespeare mean when he drew the character of Hamlet?" This is a question about the goal of art, not its structure, and can only be answered by attentive listening to the character. The best criticism of Johnson, Hazlitt, Leavis, and Eliot himself is recovery of the power of art by careful observation. But because a hermeneutics of recovery is weak in methodology and rigor, it is always in danger of being nothing more than impressionism, not because the engagement with a poem is subjective, but because we have so little understanding of how poetic language works.

Responses to *The Waste Land* which fall into a hermeneutics of recovery tend to go little beyond impressionism, often describing the poem accurately (unlike some structuralist interpretations) but not explaining much about it. One of the earliest reviews of the poem, Conrad Aiken's "Anatomy of Melancholy," is an apt phenomenological description of the poem's "emotional value." Aiken dismisses the allusions and references as "unintelligible but suggestive" and concludes "that the poem succeeds—as it brilliantly does—by virtue of its incoherence, not of its plan; by virtue of its ambiguities, not of its explanations."[26] This review is characteristic of many responses to *The Waste Land*. Ezra Pound and Hugh Kenner both insist that the poem works even though the reader may have little or no knowledge of the mythical or literary origins of many of the lines and images. For Pound, the poem is "an emotional unit." Kenner quotes Eliot's own skepticism about source hunting: "I regret having sent so many enquirers off on a wild goose chase after Tarot cards and the Holy Grail." Instead, Eliot wishes the reader "would endeavor to grasp what the poetry is aiming to be . . . to grasp its entelechy."[27] Eliot is asking for a recovery of wholeness and meaning, but he clearly sees the inadequacy of subjectivism.

26. Conrad Aiken, "An Anatomy of Melancholy," in Martin (ed.), *A Collection of Critical Essays*, 58.
27. Kenner, *Invisible Poet*, 151–52.

Eliot himself emphasized the need for rigor and discipline in impressionistic criticism: "The moment you try to put the impressions into words, you either begin to analyze and construct, to *'eriger en lois,'* or you begin to create something else."[28] Eliot insists upon the need for an analysis which does not violate the integrity of the whole and a construction which does not create something else. For Eliot, analysis, the tool of suspicion and demystification, goes hand in hand with a positive movement of construction that does not create a new object, but recovers the present one. Eliot suggests a dialectic in criticism, which Ricoeur, also, concludes is necessary. Most recently, Ricoeur has replaced the terms "hermeneutics of suspicion" and "hermeneutics of recovery" with the terms "explanation" and "understanding," possibly out of an unwillingness to allow the techniques of suspicion to constitute a true hermeneutic in themselves. For Ricoeur, the moment of understanding and recovery should always precede and, indeed, encompass the work of suspicion and explanation. Only attentive listening can lead the work of explanation in the right direction.[29]

The tools of phenomenology can help us only partially. A case in point is the excellent recent article by William Spanos, "Repetition in *The Waste Land*: A Phenomenological De-struction." The article makes a convincing case against the interpretations of the poem which emphasize spatiality, irony, and myth:

> Eliot's strategy is broadly assumed to involve the reflexive or "ironic" juxtaposition of past and present, mythic and contemporary image, from a teleological vantage point in order to negate temporal—and "interested"—hermeneutic encounter with the poem in favor of a logocentrically simultaneous or spatial—and "objective"—perception. It is also assumed to have its ultimate motive in either Eliot's privileged metaphysics of presence, his awareness of the spiritually limiting condition of historical time, or, if the critic

28. T. S. Eliot, *The Sacred Wood* (London, 1928), 5.
29. Paul Ricoeur, *Interpretation Theory: Discourse and the Surplus of Meaning* (Fort Worth, 1976), 71–88.

> is hostile, in his radical contempt or disgust for the world and in his nostalgic desire to annihilate its contingent motion to achieve the certain stillness of the eternal moment.[30]

Spanos challenges those assumptions with an interpretation of the poem which is radically temporal; for him, the poem is a progression in which a central protagonist learns to accept, or more accurately, to appropriate time, finitude, and uncertainty partly through an existential understanding of the cycle of life and death referred to in the myths and allusions. The protagonist and the reader are denied stability, certitude, and a sense of closure (presence) by the poem itself, thus keeping them open to authentic being, which is based on death and open-endedness (absence). This excellent phenomenological insight into the poem is a step beyond the sketchiness of Aiken or Pound and is the result of much careful observation of the poem, such as his sensitive reading of Tiresias: "The visually oriented critics who have said or implied that Tiresias' ability to foresee and to foresuffer . . . is a manifestation of his liberating spatial consciousness have not *listened* to the diminishing strain of futile pathos that pervades the lines which reveal their terrible knowledge." But Spanos' discussion remains at a very general level of insight; he still cannot explain much of the detail of the poem except by explaining every difficult or ambiguous passage as a reference to existential ambiguity. The article is also typically phenomenological in seeing the poem as the conscious experience of a protagonist, which is, I believe, a distortion of the poem. For example, Spanos interprets each section of *The Waste Land* as representing a season which connects to the fertility and Grail myths. But he also conscientiously admits:

> For the fact is that in discovering the "plot" I have, of course, tended to cover over, to conceal, the ambiguities that *may* be discontinuities in the poem: that, for example, there are references to other than the initially established season in four of the five sections and to the phases of the fertility ar-

30. Spanos, "Repetition in *The Waste Land*," 227–28.

> chetypes and Grail legend in other than the *expected* place
> in the seasonal pattern. . . . They constitute, in Edward Said's
> apt terms, a molestation of the protagonist's and thus of our
> authority.[31]

Spanos understands that the meaning he sees in *The Waste Land*—the seasonal quest of a narrator—is to some degree distorting the particulars of the poem. Like virtually every critic of *The Waste Land*, he assumes the presence of a central persona and this assumption makes him unable to account for much of the poem even though he is phenomenologically aware that the poem is speaking to him from beyond the horizon of his explanation. So, while the article is generally illuminating, and, to my mind, a necessary reinterpretation of the poem, it also reveals the limits of phenomenological interpretation which does not put the subject in question.

While I will insist that true art always speaks to us from beyond our horizon, I also believe that interpretation of *The Waste Land* is particularly far afield when tied to the ideas of persona and dualist epistemology. Spanos sees how central the communication of absence is, but he doesn't know how to account for the poem's density. There is more than simply death in those absences; there is also life as we know it, that is, dense with possibility. The individual submission to finitude is also a cultural explosion into infinite change. Spanos' existential bias makes him limit the poem's possibilities to an existential allegory of finitude.

In summary, while both structural and phenomenological interpretations, both suspicion and recovery, have yielded insightful close readings of moments in *The Waste Land*, the opacity of the poem remains. To do full justice to this opacity, we must find a way to account for its densities and its absences. The great philosophic enterprise of the twentieth century—the attempt to see the universe in linguistic terms—provides just such a way.

---

31. *Ibid.*, 254, 263.

Chapter Two

The Hermeneutic
Universe ■

Objects cannot arise without names, and names never spring up without objects.

T. S. Eliot
Knowledge and Experience

I

Hugh Kenner, discussing the *symboliste* heritage of Eliot and Pound, writes "Eliot's line has no lost structure to restore, as the searcher after 'meaning' soon discovers. . . . Pound omits, omits, but knows what he is omitting and can restore on demand, but behind Eliot's resonances there is frequently nothing to restore."[1] Insofar as this statement is true, it is Eliot, rather than Pound, who has transcended romantic nostalgia for unity. Eliot's world exists in the words of the poem, not in any experience of the poet, as Kenner thinks is the case with Pound. Kenner is arguing that Eliot remains a symbolist, creating poems that incarnate an otherwise ineffable mystical or emotional experience. But the truth of Kenner's statement that there is nothing to restore behind Eliot's lines is a more radical truth than can be accounted for in symbolist

1. Hugh Kenner, *The Pound Era* (Berkeley, 1971), 132–33.

terms; however, the symbolist aesthetic provides an instructive starting point for our inquiry.

The French symbolists, arch-romantics though some of them were, initiated a new being of the word which was to lead poetry both deeper into and finally out of subjectivism. The symbolists attempted to detach the word from both things and ideas, freeing it to express "ineffable" spiritual and emotional states. The word became valued for connotative rather than denotative meaning and was forced further and further from empirical reference or rational meaning. For those late romantics, the world, dispossessed of God, man, and finally language, becomes meaningless, fragmented, dead—an object for scientific study, nothing more. A subjective or transcendent world was the only possible province of poetry.[2]

The twentieth-century poetic response to this nihilism, as J. Hillis Miller has termed it, has been to move back to a reality of meaningful physical things.[3] Nevertheless, language has been forever altered by the symbolists' experiments. Divorced from reference, language gains an autonomous power that has vastly influenced twentieth-century poetry. Words no longer merely point to the meaningful thing; words can evoke experiences not available in any other form. In this way the symbolists gave us a richer understanding of what might constitute "reality." Theirs was a reality not circumscribed by empirical or rational boundaries; they asserted the priority of emotional and spiritual states of being. But the symbolist detachment of word from thing also eventually must undermine the attachment of word to personal emotion or transcendent spirituality. The power resides in the word, not in any reference to a preexisting, ineffable state.

These two consequences of symbolist thought—the autonomy of the word and the expansion of reality—have spawned in our century two types of rejection of romanticism and return to reality.

2. See Arthur Symons, *The Symbolist Movement in Literature* (London, 1908), and Edmund Wilson, *Axel's Castle* (New York, 1931), for studies of the symbolist movement.
3. This is Miller's thesis in *Poets of Reality*, hereinafter cited parenthetically in the text as PR.

Hillis Miller in *Poets of Reality* brilliantly defines one line of this dissent, epitomized in the work of William Carlos Williams. Williams, says Miller, tries to strip language of subjectivizing properties in order to merge language with the thing itself. Rejecting figurative language almost totally, shunning tradition, artifice, and convention as much as possible, Williams strives for union with the thing, yet always respecting language as a thing in itself. Williams works to write a language as pure and clear as the thing in order to express a union which seems to exist prior to language: "things have no names for me," he declares.[4] The objective world is remarkably *present* for Williams. Even though he acknowledges the mystery of the thing, the poetry suggests an utter security in his union with reality. Miller cites "a strange lack of tension" (PR, 288) in Williams' work, due to a total lack of romantic dualism.

Miller sees modern poetry as resolving dualism in a unitary physical reality which includes both man and nature. The "reality" referred to in his book's title is not the same reality as perceived by the symbolists. Miller's odd interpretation of Eliot reveals the nature of this reality even more clearly. For Miller, Eliot remains imprisoned in subjectivity until his conversion to Christianity, when "a time ordered by God rather than by man" releases him into reality (PR, 184). In Eliot's later poetry, Miller argues, Eliot reveals an appreciation for the physical world which is lacking in the early poetry, for in the early poetry the world was meaningless and in the later it holds God's immanence. Thus, the early poetry is always subjectivizing a reality which finally can be known only through God, who informs the concrete moment with the "radiant presence of the present" (PR, 189).

Miller cites images from "Ash Wednesday" to show Eliot's "return from idealist isolation to a physical world": "The lost lilac and the lost sea voices"; "the bent golden-rod and the lost sea smell"; "the cry of the quail and the whirling plover"; "the salt savour of

4. William Carlos Williams, *Selected Letters*, ed. John C. Thirlwall (New York, 1957), 147.

the sandy earth" (PR, 185). But Miller's argument can be countered by the symbolists' redefinition of the nature of language and reality.

Even taken out of context, the images Miller cites do more than correspond to physical reality because of the poetic self-reflexivity of rhythm and alliteration and also because of the human affect introduced by a word like "lost." Even a very referential image like "the cry of the quail and the whirling plover" is charged with a human consciousness of the object. Because of the independence of words from reference, "cry" retains its affective connotation, even though it is a cliché to describe a recognizable object. And the juxtaposition of a "cry" and a "whirling" bird triggers the always active metaphoricity of our malleable language; the whirling becomes affected by sadness rather than by fury or speed, and the cry itself is taken up in winding motion rather than heard in a stillness. This image is not mere objective reality, but is reality understood in a human way, no more objective than subjective.

In context the image is even less objective. This passage from the last section of "Ash Wednesday" enacts a recovery of the sea which is highly charged with symbolic significance involving cleansing, baptism, and renewal. The "cry of the quail" is echoed fewer than twenty lines later in the last line of the poem: "And let my cry come unto Thee," while the "whirling plover" echoes the previous section in which "Against the Word the unstilled world still whirled." Rather than representing a return to the physical world, this image becomes part of an allegory of spiritual quest for a transcendent state.

Only in a very conventional sense can we continue to believe that the images cited by Miller seem less subjective than an early image such as "The river's tent is broken; the last fingers of leaf / Clutch and sink into the wet bank" (The Waste Land). This image forcefully presents reality coming to language in a human interpretation, but I would not see such images as Miller does, as "aspects of the solitary self" (PR, 185). Even though death by drowning is a motif of The Waste Land, this particular image does not get absorbed into an allegory as the later image from "Ash Wednesday" does. Rather, the affective quality of the world is being invoked as autumn, death, and desperation are brought forth.

It is odd that Miller should equate the reality of God with Williams' non-transcendent reality. They are surely not similar except in a certain attitude of serenity. Eliot, in the late poetry, is more optimistic about the possibility for beauty and love than he is in the early work. But trying to show the presence of God in the particular is no more concrete than trying to show the absence of God in the particular. Miller's definition of reality as a merging of self and world in the present and luminous relegates all opacity and ugliness to the ghetto of subjectivity. The Christian world of Eliot is a world that is taken care of; it is, to a large degree, ordered and serene, if only one can lose oneself in the concrete particulars. But it is a world far removed from many realities.

There is another notion of reality revealed in twentieth-century literature which was first suggested by the symbolists, then defined by a few poems of Eliot, Stevens, late Williams (particularly in "Paterson"), and remains strongly evident in the recent poems of John Ashbery. In these poets, dualism is dissolved in language, not merely, as Pound thought, in the language of poets "whose clean perception sets realities before the mind,"[5] but in the very nature of language. For these poets, the world as we know it is given to us in language. Eliot learned from F. H. Bradley that an immediate experience of the world, the experience Williams claims when he says, "I feel as much a part of things as trees and stones,"[6] is not available to us. According to Eliot, immediate experience "is a timeless unity which is not as such present either anywhere or to anyone."[7] And, in spite of Williams' assertions to the contrary, his poetry often seems to be referring to an experience which is not in the poem because it cannot be in language at all.

5. Kenner, *Pound Era*, 141.
6. Williams, *Selected Letters*, 147.
7. T. S. Eliot, *Knowledge and Experience in the Philosophy of F. H. Bradley* (New York, 1964), 31. This book will be discussed at length in Chapter Three.

If all that we can know is language, then there is an equalizing of object, perception, feeling, and thought as linguistic constructions and a broadening of reality to include all linguistic artifacts—books, plays, songs, etc. The linguistic world is much denser than the world of luminous particulars, because so much more is available to it. And this linguistic world is constantly metamorphosing since it is not referentially attached to one thing or experience, but is infinitely responsive to changes.

What the symbolists took for the richness of their own minds or souls could be seen as the result of liberating language from the prison of reference and allowing it to play. I would argue that their poems no more refer to a transcendent mystical experience than to the empirical world. The power of their unexpected juxtapositions is not in a Platonic unity of all things, but in the malleable nature of language. When language no longer is connected to an unchanging or infinite object, then its own finite, changing nature gives the poem great power in infinite possibilities for new speaking. And each new speaking is not merely a subjective point of view on a fixed object, not just the alienation of impressionism; the linguistic creation has an ontological status equal to the object. A new being is uncovered and has found its way into our world. Mallarmé's "golden galleys, beautiful as swans, / sleeping on a river of crimson and fragrance"[8] embodies more than an affective state.

Why is it necessary to speak in this way, to place in the realm of reality poetry which is traditionally known as anti-realist? I do not wish to blur literary distinctions. But I do wish to point up the fact that most critical assumptions about poetic meaning are based on a reference theory of meaning in which words refer to an *a priori* reality. And if the poetic image conforms to certain conventions of realism, it is thought to refer to this reality or to the rational consciousness of the lyric poem. If it does not conform to those conventions, it is then seen as the creation of a subjective state. Since *The Waste Land* clearly rejects the conventions of logic, causality,

8. Stéphane Mallarmé, *Selected Poems*, trans. C. F. MacIntyre (Berkeley, 1965), 9.

and rationality, its meaning is assumed to be based in a subjective, even solipsistic emotional state.

Twentieth-century Anglo-American poetic theory is steeped in reference theories of meaning. I. A. Richards' division of meaning into emotive and referential categories remained influential long after Richards himself developed a more sophisticated contextual theory of meaning.[9] The effect of assigning poetry to emotive meaning over against referential meaning is to deny any ontological status to poetry, while finding value mainly in psychological states. Richards' fascination with the malleability and metaphoricity of poetic language initially leads him to draw this distinction; how could such shifting, connotative, "ambiguous" language refer to any "truth" in the way that scientific language does?

John Crowe Ransom's rebuttal of Richards is instructive. He would like an ontological approach which emphasizes the truth which is in the poem and not in the reader's psyche. But at the same time, he must deny the malleability of language to form new wholes from disparate parts. For Ransom, unity can be achieved only with logic, not with mere juxtaposition of images. Ransom writes: "My belief is that opposites can never be said to be resolved or reconciled merely because they have been got into the same poem, or got into the same complex of affective experience to create there a kind of 'tension'; that if there is a resolution at all it must be a logical resolution."[10] Ransom is trying to preserve some "proper" meaning for words, so that they can be used in the service of objective truth. But even Ransom succumbs to a psychological duality similar to that of Richards in his distinction between structure and texture, the former carrying a rational meaning and the latter an irrational meaning.[11] The "improper" richness of poetic language is not lost on Ransom the poet, though it cannot be justified in his ontology.

9. I. A. Richards, *Principles of Literary Criticism* (1924; rpr. London, 1930), 267.

10. John Crowe Ransom, *The New Criticism* (New York, 1941), 95.

11. William K. Wimsatt and Cleanth Brooks, *Literary Criticism: A Short History* (New York, 1957), 629–30.

Richards, too, found his early arguments one-sided and restricting for poetry. In *The Philosophy of Rhetoric* he develops a contextual theory of meaning which denies "proper" meaning to all language.[12] In this theory, meaning does not belong to a word; words have no meaning except in the context of discourse as a whole. Even in the most unambiguous language, meaning is determined by convention and context. And in poetic language, the word is freed from convention to inhabit strange new contexts and create new meanings. Richards' idea of context is very close to the idea of a diacritical system of signs, but he does not address the problem of how this sign system gets invested with semantic value. Richards' semantics, according to Paul Ricoeur, "ignores the duality of a theory of signs and a theory of the instance of discourse, and builds directly on the thesis of the interanimation of words in the living utterance."[13] Richards' explanation of how we are to interpret poetry reveals the weakness in his argument. We must not, says Richards, be tied to conventional interpretation because,

> Its evil is that it takes the senses of an author's words to be things we know before we read him, fixed factors with which he has to build up the meaning of his sentences as a mosaic is put together of discrete independent tesserae. Instead, they are resultants which we arrive at only through the interplay of the interpretive possibilities of the whole utterance. In brief, we have to guess them and we guess much better when we realize we are guessing and watch out for indications, than when we think we know.[14]

If interpretation is to proceed by guesswork, then the ontological status of the poem seems to have little force of its own. The psychological tendency remains. William Empson, who follows Richards in his desire for semantic richness, has a similar dependence

---

12. I. A. Richards, *The Philosophy of Rhetoric* (New York, 1965), 28–40.

13. Paul Ricoeur, *The Rule of Metaphor: Multi-disciplinary Studies of the Creation of Meaning in Language*, trans. Robert Czerny with Kathleen Mac-Laughlin and John Costello (Toronto, 1977), 79.

14. Richards, *The Philosophy of Rhetoric*, 55.

on the reader's response: "Which class [of ambiguity] any particular poem belongs to depends in part on your own mental habits and critical opinions."[15]

Clearly, what is needed is a way to ground ontologically the contextual/diacritical view of language if we are not to be trapped in linguistic relativism or solipsism. This was, I believe, a project of Eliot's, though the language of his criticism is so similar to that of other New Critics that it is difficult to see how different some of his perspectives are. For this reason, I would like to explore in the remainder of this chapter some possible philosophical solutions to the problems outlined above, before turning to Eliot's own philosophical work. Philosophy may help us find a ground for meaning which is not an ahistorical consciousness, but is profoundly historical and non-subjective, or, in our previous terms, a ground which maintains the finitude and malleability of language along with an ontological "presence."

What if, for example, the word is autonomous as the symbolists wished? But if the word is not connected to the thing, must we discard reference to the world altogether in favor of either a Platonic idea or a solipsistic, linguistic creation? Or perhaps could we see the world in a different way, a way that would make reference and meaning possible *because* of the autonomy of words and make the autonomy of the word an essential element in the nature of reality?

In other words, what ontology is implied by the style of *The Waste Land*? If there is "nothing behind" Eliot's images in terms of a corresponding reference and if an essentialist structure of reference seems particularly inadequate for this poem, then where does meaning lie? It has been the great project of this century to understand meaning as not based on essences or reference. This project has produced two separate but clearly related possibilities for meaning, which I will designate diacritical meaning and hermeneutic meaning. The first results from a study of sign systems and sometimes seems to offer an inadequate embrace of the possibilities of the world. The second includes the first in many ways but

15. William Empson, *Seven Types of Ambiguity* (New York, 1947), 57.

deepens the analysis. In hermeneutics we find an ontology which preserves meaning in the absence of self.

II

The linguistic turn in twentieth-century philosophy, which is the basis for my preceding comments, has not been fully absorbed by literary theory. Literary critics, no doubt feeling that their attention has always been turned to language, have often ignored many of the implications of recent thought for literary interpretation. Therefore, even though this linguistic turn has been more thoroughly and competently described elsewhere, I feel it necessary to outline the philosophical coherence of those ideas which for me both necessitate and result from a rereading of *The Waste Land*.

The linguistic turn may be summarized in a general way by Ferdinand de Saussure's great realization that language is an arbitrary and diacritical system of culture which does not reflect meaning but determines meaning.[16] Saussure's rethinking of language coincides with the work of such demystifiers as Heidegger, Freud, Marx, and Nietzsche: to destruct the metaphysics of the self by finding that humans are controlled by forces other than the conscious self, such as culture, or the unconscious, or language. As a result, if the self is determined by language and language is determined by culture and culture is surely a human creation, then there is a lack of groundedness here—a continual deferral of the origin of meaning. This sense of deferral is at the heart of my discussion of absence in *The Waste Land*.

My discussion of Saussure and diacritical meaning will be brief, since they have been so often summarized. But I do wish to highlight the linguistic absence which Saussure suggests and which has

16. Ferdinand de Saussure, *Course in General Linguistics*, trans. Wade Baskin, ed. Charles Bally and Albert Sechehaye (New York, 1959). This discovery is also at the heart of the ordinary language philosophy growing out of Wittgenstein and Peirce.

been overlooked by some of his immediate critical successors in structuralism and formalism. Saussurean linguistics offers a clear refutation of traditional theories of meaning that see words as somehow attached to preexisting referents in the world or to ideas in the mind. Saussure began with the definition of language as a system of signs and proceeded to analyze the sign into the by now familiar signifier and signified. Though these terms roughly correspond to form and content, they are actually both elements of form.[17] In fact, Saussure's most revolutionary work concerns what is signified by the sign.

The signifier offers little trouble; it is the clearly arbitrary form, varying from language to language, and is distinguished phonetically in relation to all the other signifiers in a language. But it is also clear from a little comparative linguistics that the signified, too, is arbitrary and does not refer to universal concepts. The most common example of this principle is the conceptual variation between the English "to know" and the French "*savoir*" and "*connaître*." Jonathan Culler gives another striking example of conceptual variation by comparing the English "river" and "stream" with the French "*fleuve*" and "*rivière*": "The signified 'river' is opposed to 'stream' solely in terms of size, whereas a 'fleuve' differs from a 'rivière' not because it is necessarily larger but because it flows into the sea, while a 'rivière' does not. In short, 'fleuve' and 'rivière' are not signifieds or concepts of English."[18] In other words, each language creates its own concepts and these concepts only have identity within a specific language system. Identity is determined diacritically, that is, relationally. In a diacritical system a word exists only in differentiation from all the other words in the system. The signified is not a fixed referent or idea in the world, but is a formal division of possible experience.

The effect of Saussure's work is to separate the sign from reference, leaving a gap between language and "reality." This gap is widened further by Saussure's distinction between *langue* and *parole*,

17. See Jonathan Culler, *Ferdinand de Saussure* (New York, 1977), 15–20.
18. *Ibid.*, 15.

langue being the language system and *parole* the actual speech act. Saussure's distinctions are helpful here: *langue* is the "hoard deposited by the practice of speech in speakers who belong to the same community, a grammatical system which, to all intents and purposes, exists in the mind of each speaker"; and *parole* is both "the combinations by which the speaker uses the code of the linguistic system in order to express his own thoughts" and "the psychological mechanisms which permit him to externalize these combinations."[19] Saussure believed that linguistics should be concerned only with *langue*, a move which further isolates language from any immediate experience of reality by removing the speaking subject of *parole*. Many structuralists have taken this second gap—that between *langue* and *parole*—much more seriously than the gap between language and reference. Later semioticians consider the absence of reference as central because language never exists in the static state of *langue* but is always in the shifting, metamorphosing mode of *parole*. Semioticians also debate among themselves the degree of distance between language and the speaking subject. In fact, the popular debate now occurring between traditional humanist critics and linguistic critics obscures the more important issues now being argued within the circles of linguistic philosphers; that is, given that language is social, relational, arbitrary, and largely determining of how we think, is there any way to retain any autonomy and creativity for the subject?

The structuralists, who were the immediate successors to Saussure, regarded texts in much the fashion of the New Critics, as self-contained objects, as machines made of words. They tried to find the *langue* of each event, text, or group of texts, sometimes ending up with overly rigid and useless formulae. The insights of the structuralists were often helpful, drawing attention to internal relationships and patterns overlooked by critics interested only in reference. But structuralists tend to be essentialists in their own way, because they see their structure as the central, essential, and ori-

---

19. Culler, *Saussure*, 22–23; Saussure, *Course*, 13–14.

ginary meaning in the text, often with no regard for any changing semantic or historical circumstances outside of the text.[20]

Finally, structural analysis founders on the fact of meaning; structuralists have given little attention to the arbitrary nature of the signified. In discourse the categories of structure, the oppositions, the patterns, cannot be discussed like mathematical entities. They must have a name, and to this problem the structuralists have given insufficient attention. In his famous analysis of *Oedipus Rex*, Levi-Strauss divides the myth into two sets of binary oppositions: over- and under-valuation of kinship relations, and affirmation and negation of man's autochthony.[21] Where do these categories come from? They are, to me, meaningful and helpful, but they presuppose a meaning prior to the structural analysis. Levi-Strauss is helpful for his intelligent insights as much as for his structuralist method. In fact, structural analysis has proved to be of little help with individual texts *unless* there is the prior engagement by the critic which shapes the analysis.[22]

The gap between sign and meaning seems to widen as you move from an act of speaking, where ostensive definition and shared intentions of communication may clarify meaning, to writing which may be divorced from both speaker and hearer. And within writing, literature, which is concerned much less than other types of writing with a particular intention of communication, gives most freedom to the amount of variance between language and meaning. A work of literature may have many meanings attached to its set of signs. Indeed the gap[23] is what allows language to be released from

---

20. Spanos, "Repetition in *The Waste Land*," links structuralism with logocentrism. Contemporary semioticians stress the need for a constant destruction and rebuilding of structures to avoid such reification.

21. Claude Levi-Strauss, "The Structural Study of Myth," in *Structural Anthropology*, trans. Claire Jacobson and Brooke Grundfest Schoepf (Garden City, N.Y., 1967), 213–16.

22. Ricoeur makes this point forcefully in *Interpretation Theory*, 86–88.

23. Jacques Derrida analyzes this difference between sign and meaning along with the constant deferral of meaning into a system of differences. For him the gap is a *differance*, a constant deferral of wholeness and origin of meaning. See "Differance," in *Speech and Phenomena*, trans. David B. Allison (Evanston, Ill., 1973), 129–160.

the restrictions of a particular speaker in a particular situation. Freeing language from a particular situation allows language to create distant, even imaginary, structures. As Ricoeur writes of this autonomy of language, "Thanks to writing, man and only man has a world and not just a situation."[24]

The freeing of language from the psychological intentions of a speaker allows the natural polysemy of language to function.[25] Even the conventional meaning of a signifier, the denotative meaning of the dictionary, often has several variations from years of use or misuse. In addition, a signifier may have connotative meaning, associations from the different contexts in which it has been used. And for the most radical linguists, a signifier may mean virtually anything. Jonathan Culler explains, "If, Saussure writes, the most precise characteristic of every sign is that it differs from other signs, then every sign in some sense bears the traces of all other signs; they are co-present with it as the entities which define it."[26] This is the basis for Julia Kristeva's genotype and Jacques Derrida's free play, both of which seek to demystify or deconstruct any one privileged definition or structure in favor of an ongoing, totally unbounded process of interpretation. In practice, of course, both *are* bound to some principle of semantic relevance, though Derrida tests his readers' imaginations by pushing semantic relevance to its limit.[27] But we must all admit that a striking new interpretation often changes our idea of what information may be relevant to a text. Saussure's theories free the word by abolishing the speaking self in favor of a play of differences among signs. As language moves from situational discourse into literature it depends more and more on these diacritical effects of absence. The problem is that once the subject is gone and a "use" theory of meaning is invalidated, it seems that you must rely on essences for meaning (as many critics do) or

24. Ricoeur, *Interpretation Theory*, 36.
25. Derrida claims that this polysemy functions in all language, even spoken language, which is why the idea of writing is primary for him. See *Of Grammatology*, trans. Gayatri Chakravorty Spivak (Baltimore, 1974).
26. Culler, *Saussure*, 122.
27. Jonathan Culler, *Structuralist Poetics: Structuralism, Linguistics, and the Study of Literature* (Ithaca, N.Y., 1975), 241–54.

be totally nihilistic about meaning as some very radical critics claim to be.

If Derrida were to take his notion of writing to the extreme, he would have no guide for relevance at all, finding meaning everywhere—even in random combinations of letters[28]—and thus, in a sense, finding meaning nowhere. For such critics, language is a ceaseless, seamless web, without origins or goals: the entropic point where the rigidity and complexity of a structure coincide with total contingency. They find a sense of freedom and exhilaration by remaining at that point where all is meaningful and nothing is meaningful, where everything is a text and therefore nothing is a privileged text. It is a rigorous anarchy, foreign to most minds, particularly that of the traditional essentialist critic.

III

This radical extension of what I am calling diacritical meaning is not a completely accurate representation of the complex and evolving theories of someone like Derrida. But his example serves to point up the need for a grounding of meaning which must not reinstate essentialism into linguistic philosophies as some structuralists do. Derrida understands the need for a grounding which can only exist under what he calls erasure: a center which is a non-center, "a rule of the game which does not govern the game." This is not just chaos or total flux anymore than it is absolute rigidity. Derrida keeps the paradox taut. The free play of language is "permitted by the lack, the absence of a center or origin," but "I didn't say that there was no center, that we could get along without the center. I believe that the center is a function, not a being—a reality, but a function. And this function is absolutely indispens-

28. Saussure was interested in anagrams in Latin poetry, and his interest has been taken up by some radical critics such as Julia Kristeva who argue that there should be no constraints whatsoever on how we interpret a text, not even the constraint of the inviolable word. This attitude does not allow the text much ontological stability. See Culler, *Structuralist Poetics*, 249–50.

able."[29] Derrida's dynamic, functioning absence moves beyond the purely linguistic paradigm of Saussure, which cannot account for the emergence of meaning. The linguistic system of sameness and difference, initially derived from the study of phonemes and words, is powerless to explain the creation of meaning at the level of the sentence or discourse where language "connects" with the world.[30] Derrida's notion of *"differance,"* though "neither a word nor a concept," nevertheless conveys both a linguistic gap between signified and signifier and, in the sense of deferral, an absence which is ontological.[31] The deferral of meaning throughout the diacritical system is propelled by and is in search of an origin which is not part of this system. But since it is not part of the system of signification, it cannot be known except as an absence or concealedness. Here, Heidegger's influence on Derrida is all important, although Derrida accuses Heidegger of a nostalgia for a lost and inarticulable presence, a "transcendental signified," while Derrida embraces an "always already absent present."[32]

I mention Derrida mainly to reach Heidegger. Even though Derrida has made great advances in the application of Heideggerian thought to semiotic ideas, Heidegger has meditated on artistic creation in a way that is not, I believe, nostalgic for a lost presence, but is historical. Linguistic questions inevitably lead to ontological ones, even as Mallarmé's injunctions about the word are connected to a Platonic notion of reality. What kind of world/being is coming to meaning in poetic language and, for the present, in the language of *The Waste Land?* If we cannot follow the *symbolistes* in their belief that the malleability of language implies a higher spiritual real-

29. Jacques Derrida, "Structure, Sign, and Play in the Discourse of the Human Sciences," in Richard Macksey and Eugenio Donato (ed.), *The Structuralist Controversy: The Languages of Criticism and the Sciences of Man* (Baltimore, 1970), 267, 260, 271.

30. "Connect" is only a provisional term, since I am trying to escape a referential theory of meaning where ideas or things are connected to words. After Heidegger, we would say that language *is* the world.

31. Derrida, "Differance," 130.

32. Gayatri Chakravorty Spivak, "Translator's Preface," *Of Grammatology,* xvi–xvii.

ity, then only Heidegger's ontology, which is a hermeneutic ontology of absence, will answer this question. Heidegger calls forth a ground for meaning which is neither transcendental (in the usual sense), nor subjective, nor empirical. Nor would I like to call it linguistic; it is better described as hermeneutic. Heidegger shows us how to gather up the lessons of diacritical linguistics into a hermeneutic theory of meaning that is invaluable for literary criticism. For while a rejection of subjectivity can be seen in the works of Marx and Freud as well as Nietzsche, they, like Saussure, replace the power of the rational mind with forces which, it can be argued, remain based in an ontology of "presence" that makes them overly restricting paradigms for the study of artistic creation and meaning, which are based in the mystery of absence.[33] Nothing less than a new ontology is necessary to understand the world called forth by *The Waste Land* or the advance Eliot made through symbolism to a radically new kind of statement and meaning.

Heidegger's student and colleague Hans-Georg Gadamer is responsible for documenting the central position of hermeneutics in Heidegger's work. Gadamer points out that for Heidegger hermeneutics is no longer a method of understanding, but is "a theory of the real experience that thinking is."[34] Interpretation or understanding "is the original character of the being of human life itself" (TM, 230). This shift from epistemology to ontology is the culmination and transformation of the hermeneutic tradition; whereas previous philosphers worked to find a ground for the truth of interpretation, Heidegger reverses the problem and makes interpretation, as a non-subjective activity, a ground for human being.

Hermeneutics has, of course, been with us for centuries, having arisen from the desire to determine the truth of God as inscribed in the Bible. Until the nineteenth century, hermeneutics remained a

33. Nietzsche is, of course, always problematical and has been interpreted and reinterpreted in many different ways. But Heidegger found that Nietzsche did not sufficiently destroy metaphysics. The reinterpretation of Freud by Lacan brings out the negativity functioning in Freudian theory.
34. Hans-Georg Gadamer, *Truth and Method* (New York, 1975), xxiv. Hereinafter cited parenthetically in the text as TM.

means to attain an absolute and objective truth. But as thinkers began to turn their attention to the human sciences such as history, psychology, sociology, and literary criticism, they realized that the rigid rules of interpretation were not adequate for the living character of human objects. In the best spirit of romanticism, Schleiermacher and Dilthey added the subjective to the hermeneutic process, making understanding a process of interaction between human subject and human object based on their common participation in "the historical consciousness of the human."[35] But, as Gadamer clearly shows (TM, 192–225), Dilthey's attempt to ground understanding in life was in conflict with his need to combat relativism by positing the possibility of an absolute historical consciousness. Likewise, Husserl's scientific attempt to begin with the life-world is undermined by the idealism inherent in his process of transcendental reduction. While both Dilthey and Husserl tried to go beyond dualism, they both finally give consciousness priority over language. In each case the search for a ground for knowledge returned to a dualist epistemology running counter to their attempts to overturn traditional metaphysics.

Only with Heidegger's work is this conflict resolved into a seamless expression of Being. For Heidegger defines human being (*Dasein* or There-Being) as an event of understanding prior to the possibility of knowledge. What was previously an object of knowledge for a subject is now "itself ultimately of the essence of There-being" (TM, 232). As Heidegger's noted commentator William Richardson explains,

> Heidegger saw that the problem had to be posed on a different level in terms of an intimate correlation between the Being-process and man, by reason of which the "sense" of beings was something more than mere entity, yet also more than the fabrication of consciousness. This would demand, however, an analysis of man in his relationship to Being that

35. David M. Rasmussen, *Mythic-Symbolic Language and Philosophical Anthropology: A Constructive Interpretation of the Thought of Paul Ricoeur* (The Hague, 1971), 12.

would shatter the realist-idealist dilemma by overcoming the subjectivism that lay at its roots.[36]

To repeat, Heidegger has changed the "sense" of beings or reality so that it is rich with human interpretation but not subjective. In other words, the process of interpretation is what *is*, not a way to reach what is. Interpretation achieves ontological status, not as a subjective process but as the *being* process.

I do not wish for Heidegger's very difficult, interpenetrating ideas to take over this discussion. Suffice it to say that what follows is a very limited presentation of those ideas in Heidegger which are, I think, relevant to the present study. One of the difficulties in discussing Heidegger is that his thought does not come apart into manageable entities, but exists as a unified moment of comprehension such that Being-in-the-world, which *is* concern *is* linguistically *is* time, resists description in a language beset by the errancy of logic, cause, and substance. Still, I will attempt a brief explantion of Heidegger based on the hermeneutic circle as a prelude to a more specifically literary discussion of poetic meaning.

Understanding the concept of the hermeneutic circle is particularly instructive with regard to Heidegger. The circle posits a relatedness that is not logical or causal, not proceeding from a valid ground to a logically valid conclusion. In the hermeneutic circle, each prior event of understanding in the circle grounds the next event at the same time that the next event is grounding the prior event. As in Ricoeur's hermeneutics of recovery, there is an initial understanding before knowledge is possible, though it is the possibility of that knowledge that provokes the immediate understanding. This paradigm of how interpretation works is no mere paradigm for Heidegger, but is the ontological ground of reality.

Early in *Being and Time* Heidegger sees in the question of the meaning of Being "a remarkable 'relatedness backward or forward'" in which "what is asked about has an essential pertinence

---

36. William J. Richardson, *Heidegger: Through Phenomenology to Thought* (The Hague, 1963), 28.

to the inquiry itself."[37] More, the relationship between ontological Being and particular or "ontic" human being invokes the hermeneutic circle in a way that hopes to overcome dualities by first addressing the issue of universals and particulars. Heidegger mediates the concept of Being and ontic beings with a human being called *Dasein* which "is ontically distinctive in that it *is* ontological"(BT, 32). As ontological, *Dasein* is not subjective even though it always belongs to a human being. Rather, *Dasein* is foundational: that anything *is* grounds the possibility of *Dasein*'s existence as comprehension that things are; but this ontological characteristic of *Dasein* allows the possibility that anything is. This statement does little justice to Heidegger's complexity, but moves us toward an understanding of the most important hermeneutic circle in Heidegger—time.

Richardson explains that "existence [*Dasein*] consists in the coming (future) of Being to a self that already is (past), rendering manifest the Being of beings with which it is concerned (present)."[38] For Heidegger this moving unity of future/past/present which is Being is time. Gadamer sees that Heidegger's argument that "being itself is time . . . burst asunder the whole subjectivism of modern philosophy" (TM, 228). For neither is the subject "present" nor is Being "present," but in our finitude we find ourselves in a multiplicity and change which gives us the desire to realize future possibilities for beings, but in realizing these possibilities we create multiplicity and change.

Let me explain the foregoing a bit more. Heidegger's revolutionary thinking about the nature of reality begins with two basic, almost simple, assumptions about human beings: that they are finite and that they somehow "always already" comprehend the world and the Being of things in it. *Dasein*'s finitude is the radical physical limit on its being which makes it always incomplete, insufficient,

37. Martin Heidegger, *Being and Time*, trans. John Macquarrie and Edward Robinson (New York, 1962), 28. Hereinafter cited parenthetically in the text as BT.
38. Richardson, *Heidegger*, 87.

and changing, in contrast with what would be an always sufficient, whole, and unmoving infinite. In its insufficiency, *Dasein* is inescapably rooted in the world, dependent on it for survival; Heidegger names this insufficiency "thrownness." And as thrown, *Dasein* must be cared for and caring about the world which supports *Dasein* in its finitude. On the other hand, because *Dasein* is always incomplete, it is always in a state of potential; *Dasein* is, indeed, a coming to be of possibilities. *Dasein*'s very finitude opens up a virtually unlimited range of possibilities for being. *Dasein*'s existence becomes an interpretative realization of infinite possibilities.

Our finitude is inescapably ourselves. But what distinguishes *Dasein* from other finite creatures is its "transcendence," a word not to be connected in this case with anything nonhistorical, essential, or metaphysical. In its finite transcendence, *Dasein* has a seemingly innate comprehension of the idea of Being as an ontological state.

This quality of *Dasein* is difficult only in its comprehensiveness. Richardson explains:

> Let us begin with an initial fact: even before posing the question, man has some comprehension of Being. No matter how dark or obscure Being itself may be to him, still in his most casual intercourse with other beings, they are sufficiently open to him that he may experience that they are, concern himself about what they are and how they are, decide about the truth of them, etc. He comprehends, somehow, what makes them what they are, sc. their Being. Again, every sentence that he utters contains an "is."[39]

According to Heidegger, *Dasein* is the privileged place where Being is revealed; but Being is only revealed as beings. Being is not a thing to be known, but is more comparable to a process, but a process only activated by *Dasein* in its comprehension of beings. That is, as *Dasein* recognizes beings as meaningful in its world, he recognizes that they *are*. *Dasein* understands the wholeness of beings, their

39. *Ibid.*, 33.

meaning in a special sense. In this way, *Dasein* understands itself as finite—a comprehension of its own totality lacking in other creatures. In turn, the finitude makes necessary its transcendent understanding of, concern about, a world, because *Dasein* is insufficient unto itself and must always be in a world, working at its unfinishedness in an equally unfinished and finite environment. In understanding its finitude *Dasein* also understands its own "transcendence": in its interpretation of the world, it *is* itself as finite transcendence—an always changing particularity.

It must be remembered that this claim of "transcendence" for *Dasein* is a phenomenological claim, not a claim about essence. Heidegger makes no attempt to explain why man might be privileged. *Dasein*'s origin may be in a divine plan or an evolutionary quirk; Heidegger is simply describing what *is*. (This is why Heidegger's ontology can be claimed by the religious and nonreligious alike.) What *is* is that *Dasein* finds itself in an always already meaningful world. The world is "ready-to-hand" as a context for us in which we do things. As Heidegger says, "we encounter [the room] not as something 'between four walls' in a geometrical spatial sense, but as equipment for residing" (BT, 98). Only a secondary step back makes the world an object apart from us to be studied, analyzed, known. Our primary existence is in intimate, immediate familiarity with a world, which is our finite transcendence or our concernful dwelling.

Further, Heidegger understands this concern or care to be the space of time: *"Temporality reveals itself as the meaning of authentic care"* (BT, 374). As temporal, *Dasein* is not some*thing*, but is a changing potentiality, a no-thing, being to death, the realization of which causes anxiety and concern (*Besorge*). Even the whole of interpretative possibilities cannot be grasped by finite human beings because of our limited and always changing perspective. *Dasein*'s inability to grasp Being as a whole Heidegger calls *Dasein*'s errancy.[40] *Dasein*'s errancy is both the concealedness, the

---

40. Martin Heidegger, "On the Essence of Truth," in *Existence and Being*, trans. R. F. C. Hull and Alan Crick (Chicago, 1949), 292–324. Hereinafter cited parenthetically in the text as ET.

mystery of Being as a whole, and *Dasein*'s preoccupation with particular beings. Because it is finite, *Dasein* must be concerned with particular beings, and through its concern, the particular beings are allowed to be. But *Dasein* forgets that it is in errancy and forgets that Being as a whole is concealed. Thus *Dasein* is led to believe that it can grasp Being as a whole. In this way, *Dasein* confuses Being with the only things it can know, beings, forgetting the "ontological difference" between Being and beings. In each knowing or *disclosure* of a being, the mystery of Being as a whole is *concealed;* in each disclosure, the possibilities for Being as a whole change. Thus *Dasein* is never closer to Being. Our only authentic goal is a recognition of the presence of concealedness, the mystery, the absence of presence.

We are back in a hermeneutic circle with disclosure and concealedness. But the circle is not a vicious one. As Heidegger writes:

> What is decisive is not to get out of the circle but to come into it in the right way. This circle of understanding is not an orbit in which any random kind of knowledge may move; it is the expression of the essential *fore-structure* of *Dasein* itself. It is not to be reduced to the level of a vicious circle, or even of a circle which is merely tolerated. In the circle is hidden a positive possibility of the most primordial kind of knowing. (BT, 195)

Only in the hermeneutic circle can we understand the concealing/revealing event which alone founds truth for Heidegger. While we can never know Being, which is the only essence of beings, we do not have to confine ourselves to a merely accurate empirical knowledge of beings. We can be aware of the interpretive process itself, which is "the 'letting-be' of what-is" (ET, 305). This non-subjective process can only be understood by seeing the absence or concealedness which always hides Being, the only essence of existence.

For Heidegger, this concealing/revealing event of truth is most evident in poetry. In his later works, after the so-called reversal or turn in his thought, Heidegger concentrates more and more on language as "the house of Being" and on poetry as the pure form of language. For Heidegger, a basic structure of *Dasein* is communicability; the always already meaningfulness of the world is grounded in its possibility for coming to language. Language is the place where the concealing/revealing event of interpretation happens. The gap between signified and signifier is our errancy; forgetting errancy is the impetus behind referential theories of meaning. It is in many ways helpful to think of language in the terms we have already established for *Dasein*, in that language has the same ontic-ontological structure that *Dasein* has, and language is a merging of subject and object in Being-in-the-world. Like *Dasein*, language is individual and human but not subjective. In the time of our concern, language shapes the world: the diacritical freedom of language allows a "letting-be" which is not a passive allowing, but an active participation which discovers "what-is" (ET, 306). In this way language is, and must be, autonomous and free, and at the same time, ontologically bound. No being exists without language and its freedom (*Dasein*'s concernful dwelling), but there is no language without a being.

Poetry is where this revealing of a new being and concealing of Being is most clearly seen. The circle of finitude and transcendence (or thrownness and projection) becomes in "The Origin of the Work of Art" a relationship between earth, as the concealing finitude, and world, as the disclosive projection.[41] This essay, in which Heidegger ponders the nature of creativity, requires quoting at length:

> The nature of art is poetry. The nature of poetry, in turn, is the founding of truth. We understand founding here in a triple sense: founding as bestowing, founding as grounding, and founding as beginning. Founding, however, is actual only in preserving. (OA, 75)

> The establishing of truth in the work is the bringing forth of

41. Martin Heidegger, "The Origin of the Work of Art," in *Poetry, Language, Thought,* trans. Albert Hofstadter (New York, 1971), 15–88. Hereinafter cited parenthetically in the text as OA.

> a being such as never was before and will never come to be again. . . . Truth is present only as the conflict between lighting [disclosing] and concealing in the opposition of world and earth. (OA, 62)

For Heidegger, poetry, the most privileged of the arts because it is language, both "bestows" and "preserves" a new truth. Ricoeur finds this same hermeneutic circle in the etymology of the word *invent*, which means both to create and to discover.[42] Heidegger uses the concept of figure and ground (*Gestalt*) to explain this concealing/revealing aspect of truth. Like a patterned carpet, any field or ground may contain a virtually unlimited number of possible figures which are indistinguishable from the ground until illuminated. But as one figure is illuminated it may consign a prior figure back to the ground, so that not only is the figure illuminated but the concealing nature of the ground is also "illuminated." For Heidegger, the ground is facticity, thrownness, finitude; in addition, it is profoundly historical, changing from moment to moment:

> The poetic projection of truth that sets itself into work as figure [Gestalt] is also never carried out in the direction of an indeterminate void. Rather, in the work, truth is thrown toward the caring preservers, that is, toward an historical group of men. What is thus cast forth is, however, never an arbitrary demand. Genuinely poetic projection is the opening up or disclosure of that into which human being as historical is already cast. (OA, 75)

Poetry illuminates a truth in such a way that its pull toward the ground is also revealed. Only in true poetic disclosure do we find concealment and thus become aware of our errancy. For the truth, as something that *is*, now contains the mystery of being a finite fact. Truth "refuses" to give itself as fully disclosed and it "dissembles" by obstructing the disclosure of others (OA, 54). If language is the disclosure of beings of our concern, poetic language is the disclo-

---

42. Ricoeur, *Rule of Metaphor*, 306.

sure of a new being which is never fully accessible to us. Poetry is like another human being as finite transcendence, never a thing which may be present at hand for observation. In its concealing/revealing structure, poetry (*Dasein*, world, language) is, to use Wallace Stevens' words from "To an Old Philosopher in Rome," "the extreme of the known in the presence of the extreme/of the unknown."

We may use the parallel hermeneutic pairs of finitude and transcendence, thrownness and projection, and earth and world as a way to think of our initial need to connect the autonomy of the word with an ontological ground for meaning, if we think of the autonomous word as thrownness and the ground of meaning as projection. The word is finite—not self-sufficient, but dependent on its relation with other words for meaning. But as finite, the word is not fixed and therefore is able to change and be available for the disclosure of *new* meanings. Disclosure is only possible because of the absence of fixed meaning. The word's meaning is its transcendence in a world which is "contextual" and hermeneutic. The world is the living instant of language in discourse.

The linguisticality of the world is not disconnected from the physical reality of life. The main lessons of hermeneutic ontology are that language is not a subjective property over against objective reality and that understanding comes from a linguistic, hermeneutic process. Because of being-in-the-world, reality is no longer substance with extension, but is also our imaginative and affective structures which place things in their relation to us. Solipsism is truly an impossibility for the finite transcendence of *Dasein*.

The hermeneutic nature of Heidegger's thought is emphasized in the work of Gadamer, who emphasizes the historical application of Heideggerian ideas. Gadamer sees that Heidegger has defined a way of knowing things in a finite (historical) world from a finite (historical) point within that world, a way which is radically different from the objective, scientific method which assumes the permanence of its object and often the permanence of the subject. After Heidegger, both the subject and the object are interpretations forming a meaningful world.

Gadamer uses the phrase "horizon of understanding" to explain how the finite historical character of our understanding may be open to new meanings. This metaphor powerfully images the finite but constantly mutating nature of our world, as with each slight movement the finite horizon of our vision moves with us. Gadamer writes:

> Just as the individual is never simply an individual, because he is always involved with others, so too the closed horizon that is supposed to enclose a culture is an abstraction. The historical movement of human life consists in the fact that it is never utterly bound to any one standpoint, and hence can never have a truly closed horizon. The horizon is, rather, something into which we move and that moves with us. Horizons change for a person who is moving. Thus the horizon of the past, out of which all human life lives and which exists in the form of tradition, is always in motion. (TM, 271)

The horizon of our world is not limited to our physical experience, but includes the awareness brought to us by the structures of our language, by the books we read, by the culture we participate in, and by the traditions carried forward in these structures. Thus our horizon extends far beyond our physical limits into the past and sometimes into other cultures, but our present situation is *always* included in our horizon. Our horizon is largely a common one; Gadamer is not at all speaking of a subjective, relative horizon. In understanding, there occurs a "fusion of horizons" (TM, 273) in which the fullness of one horizon is assimilated to another, thus changing both. In understanding, we can never take ourselves out of our horizon and put ourselves into a totally different horizon, as some historical thinkers wish to do. We can only understand from where we are: "we regain the concepts of an historical past in such a way that they also include our own comprehension of them" (TM, 337). And our comprehension of anything is shaped by the past as it is maintained in tradition.

For Gadamer it is an "effective historical consciousness" which understands the relation between the interpreter and the historical event or text as a hermeneutic one:

> Every historian and literary critic must reckon with the fundamental non-definitiveness of the horizon in which his understanding moves. Historical tradition can be understood only by being considered in its further determinations resulting from the progress of events. Similarly, the literary critic, who is dealing with poetic or philosophical texts, knows that they are inexhaustible. In both cases it is the progress of events that brings out new aspects of meaning in historical material. Through being re-actualized in understanding, the texts are drawn into a genuine process in exactly the same way as are the events themselves through their continuance. This is what we describe as the effective-historical element within the hermeneutic experience. (TM, 336)

Twenty years before *Truth and Method*, the principle of effective history was stated more simply when Eliot wrote, in "Tradition and the Individual Talent," "The past [is] altered by the present as much as the present is directed by the past." Effective historical consciousness is the understanding that interpretations of texts are not *mere* interpretations of static texts. The text *is* its interpretation in the present time, though that interpretation is guided by past interpretations. It is conceivable that, through time, a text may cease altogether to have meaning in the world. But it will not then be missed, for it won't even be known. The text will have no being when it has no interpretation.

What have we learned about poetry from all of this? While Heidegger's comments on poetry would be applicable to all poems from the back projection of our effective historical consciousness, there seem to be some poems which have no other explanatory reference than that of a hermeneutic ontology. As in all eras, the facticity of the twentieth century has given rise to art which is mirrored by the speculative thought of its philosophers. These are poems which disclose a world which is not substance but is linguistic interpretation. Thus in the poem, people, objects, feelings, images, symbols, myth, literature, all are ontologically equal as the horizon of the poem, as things revealed to us, but also as concealing themselves and distorting others. Logic and causality are necessarily rejected in the temporal deferral of wholeness and presence. Language emphasizes its own autonomy, malleability, and mystery as a thing. Tradition is acknowledged, not denied. Absence and possibility are offered as one.

Such poems cannot be approached—or heard—without a leap into the hermeneutic circle. They are not striving for ironic inclusiveness, a view of the whole circle, but for a finite historical moment, which is an event of interpretation. In light of this finitude and contextuality, the task of the critic is not to make educated guesses at meaning, as Richards suggests, but to see the undetermined possibilities of the poem as the key to true understanding. For it is the poem most rigidly determined which is most likely to be lost to us through time, requiring us to guess at its possible significance. The poem dense with possibility will speak to us over the years, remaining a rich and opaque ground offering up figure after figure to the light of our desire. But in understanding, we must understand that dark ground of the hermeneutic universe.

Chapter Three

Philosophy ■
Without Absolutes ■

■■■■■■■■ Any assertion about the *world*, or any *ultimate* statement
about any *object in* the world, will inevitably be an interpretation.

T. S. Eliot
Knowledge and Experience

I

Being and Time was written between the years 1916,
the year Eliot finished his dissertation on Bradley, and 1927, the year
Eliot was received into the Church of England. Given our general
acceptance of the notion of *Zeitgeist*, we are not surprised when
George Steiner writes: "Thus there is a distinct sense in which *Sein
und Zeit*, for all its erratic singularity, does belong to the same cli-
mate of catastrophe and the same quest for alternative vision as do
T. S. Eliot's *The Waste Land* or Hermann Hesse's *Blick ins Chaos*
with which it is so nearly contemporary."[1] We can, of course, make

---

1. George Steiner, *Martin Heidegger* (New York, 1978), 76.
Other coincidences concerning Heidegger and Eliot are striking, if trivial and
inevitable given their shared modernity. Each was born on September 26, though
one year apart (Eliot in 1888 and Heidegger in 1889); each finished his doctoral
dissertation in 1916; each spent time at Marburg University, where Eliot went
to study in 1914 (he did not stay long—war broke out and he went to England),
and where Heidegger taught from 1922 to 1928.

the same claim about the "erratic singularity" of *The Waste Land*, and in fact it is a critical commonplace to write of the *Zeitgeist* of modernism embracing all the arts throughout the Western world. But because the influence of Heidegger and Saussure has been so strong in shaping contemporary thought, we tend to forget that they too, are modernists. Jonathan Culler, in his book on Saussure, writes that "Saussure's theory of language is an exceptionally clear expression of the formal strategies by which a whole series of disciplines, from physics to painting, transformed themselves in the late nineteenth and early twentieth centuries and became modern. The strategy can be stated most simply as a shift in focus, from objects to relations."[2] Likewise, Heidegger's thought forms a statement of modernism that, I believe, we see mirrored in a very unlikely place—Eliot's criticism.

But Eliot's prose writings between 1916 and 1927 have not been allowed to mirror their own time. Instead, Eliot's thought is discovered to be eighteenth-century classicist or nineteenth-century idealist or medieval Christian. If we think in terms of the intellectual movements of these years, it is clear that Eliot is less easily categorized than other prominent New Critics, most of whom speak in the idiom of 1920s American pragmatism or humanism.[3] Eliot's prose writings emphasize his disagreement with pragmatism and his revulsion at the widespread British analytic movement begun by Bertrand Russell and G. E. Moore. While he identifies with T. E. Hulme's classicism and Irving Babbitt's didactic humanism, as opposed to more liberal humanism, his criticism and poetry seem bewilderingly nontraditional, nondidactic, even romantic to many readers. In his doctoral thesis, he specifically rejects, as does Bradley, the metaphysical mainstream from Descartes to Kant to Hegel, but he also, in very important ways, rejects Bradley's idealist alternative. In these years Eliot seems to be a thinker without a meta-

---

2. Culler, *Saussure*, 126.

3. However, John Crowe Ransom describes himself as specifically Neo-Hegelian and, later, Kantian. See Lewis Freed, *T. S. Eliot: The Critic as Philosopher* (West Lafayette, Ind., 1979), xvi.

physics, though his powerful criticism suggests a very firm hold on the world, indeed.

There has been a resistance among literary critics to seeing Eliot as a philosophically consistent thinker in his critical and artistic endeavors. The power of Eliot's achievement does little to dissuade critics from believing in what Ransom calls Eliot's "theoretical innocence."[4] Kenner, like many critics, finds particular value in the incidental nature of Eliot's criticism, distrusting, in typical American pragmatic fashion, the distorting lens of theory.[5] What these critics see in Eliot's criticism is his remarkable attention to the object of his inquiry, the grace and non-technical nature of his language, and the wide, non-abstract range of his interests.

But if we are to agree that every writer's style implies a metaphysics which can be unearthed, then surely every writer's ideas also imply a metaphysics. As I will argue, the only philosophy that sufficiently encompasses all of Eliot's work on this period is what we have called a hermeneutic ontology, similar to that being developed contemporaneously by Heidegger.

Although the most obvious arguments for this claim come from a reevaluation of Eliot's thesis on Bradley, the most compelling come from the criticism and, finally, the poetry. In all cases, Eliot shows himself as a man in the middle, trying to resolve the dichotomies of subject and object, idealism and realism, romanticism and classicism. His ideas stress the impersonal and objective, but his poetry, and often his criticism, suggest a deeply subjective and emotive bias. Always, Eliot is holding extremes together in a profound phenomenological recognition that neither extreme is sufficient but neither is expendable, and there is no absolute ground on which to stand in judgment. The key to his thought, particularly in this preconversion period, is his complete rejection of the idea of a self, a rejection based not, as some commentators insist, on psychological grounds, but on philosophical grounds. This deeply held

---

4. Ransom, *The New Criticism*, 145.
5. Kenner, *Invisible Poet*, 102.

philosophical conviction keeps Eliot open to paradox, humble before the other, and liberal in a personal sense even as he identifies more and more with conservative institutions. In his prose writings this rejection of self leads him to conclusions which are clearly hermeneutic in the circular grounding of seeming opposites in each other. I do not believe that Eliot abandons this hermeneutic understanding after he joins the Church of England, particularly in regard to aesthetics. But I would like to confine my analysis to Eliot's prose in years surrounding *The Waste Land,* beginning with the philosophical writings of 1916, then in the next chapter concentrating on the critical foundations of his early essays—particularly "Tradition and the Individual Talent" (1919)—as a direct aesthetic application of the philosophy.

II

There are still very few critics who are willing to take seriously Eliot's dissertation *Knowledge and Experience in the Philosophy of F. H. Bradley*[6] as a key to Eliot's thought, and only one of these has attempted, not entirely successfully in my view, to connect this document with *The Waste Land.*[7] This neglect is due in large part to the fact that the dissertation was not published until 1964, when criticism of *The Waste Land* was dominated by the great early studies. But the slight attention that the thesis has received can also be explained by Eliot's own dismissal of it:

> Forty-six years after my academic philosophizing came to an end, I find myself unable to think in the terminology of this essay. Indeed, I do not pretend to understand it. As phi-

6. Hereinafter cited parenthetically in the text as KE.
7. Bolgan's *What the Thunder Really Said* seems to concentrate more on Bradley than on Eliot's dissertation. For this reason I believe that her book misinterprets *The Waste Land,* finding it a failure in terms of a philosophy which does not reflect Eliot's thought in 1922. Other critics who attempt to use the dissertation in some way include Kenner, *Invisible Poet,* Miller, *Poets of Reality,* Freed, *Critic as Philosopher,* Smidt, *Poetry and Belief,* and Mowbray Allan, in *T. S. Eliot's Impersonal Theory of Poetry* (Lewisberg, 1974).

> losophizing, it may appear to most modern philosophers to
> be quaintly antiquated. I can present this book only as a
> curiosity of biographical interest, which shows, as my wife
> observed at once, how closely my own prose style was
> formed on that of Bradley and how little it has changed in
> all these years. (KE, 10–11)

Even those critics most interested in the thesis follow Eliot's lead
in claiming lack of understanding: Richard Wollheim, a Bradley
scholar, finds the dissertation "a painfully obscure work,"[8] and
Lewis Freed, whose book traces Bradley in Eliot's criticism, finds
that "the dissertation reads like 'Greek.'"[9] Most critics, like Anne
Bolgan (who first discovered the thesis) resort to Bradley for explanation of the thesis, sometimes, in my opinion, overlooking the
difference between Eliot and Bradley by finding Eliot's work only
an obscure explanation of Bradley, when Eliot is manifestly developing his own ideas. In fact, there has been to my knowledge no
systematic attempt to distinguish ideas in Eliot's thesis from those
of Bradley.

Less philosophically minded critics tend to misuse or dismiss the
philosophy altogether. Kristian Smidt admits that Eliot's Impersonal theory of poetry "seems to owe something to [Bradley's] *Appearance and Reality*," but "it would seem that [it] at least partly
originated in a revulsion from his own emotional freight at the time,
and an intense distrust of the private and individual personality."[10]
As Freed points out, this "shyness theory" has been more conge-
nial to most critics than the complex arguments of *Knowledge and
Experience*.[11] Bolgan, at the end of her book, writes:

> When various accounts of the Bradley/Eliot relation have
> been developed in a philosophically reliable manner, as is
> the case with [R. W.] Church, Freed, and Wollheim, they

8. Richard Wollheim, "Eliot and Bradley: An Account," in Graham Martin
(ed.), *Eliot in Perspective: A Symposium* (London, 1970), 170.

9. Freed, *Critic as Philosopher*, xvii.

10. Smidt, *Poetry and Belief*, 162, 42. Quoted in Freed, *Critic as Philosopher*,
46–47.

11. Freed, *Critic as Philosopher*, 47.

> have tended—and almost in proportion to their skill and
> exactitude—to be virtually unintelligible to the general
> reader and peripheral, therefore, to the more nearly prac-
> tical concerns of the literary critic. When, on the other hand,
> the accounts have been written by those whose orienta-
> tion is primarily literary, as is the case with Smidt, Kenner,
> and Miller, the results are sometimes not only elementary
> but inaccurate and misleading as well.[12]

To remedy this situation, attention needs to be focused on Eliot
alone as a serious poet-philosopher. Bradley's work and Eliot's work
must be distinguished, not, as Bolgan suggests, because Eliot was
religious and Bradley was not, but because Eliot makes some crucial changes in Bradley's subjective idealism, the first and foremost
of which is to deny the reality of the subjective. Eliot's thesis is difficult, but not because of obscurity; though complicated, the rea-
soning in the book is coherent. Josiah Royce called it "the work of
an expert" (KE, 10).

The difficulty of Eliot's thesis is dual. First, he is involved in an
ongoing debate with his contemporaries in which the meaning of
the issues and terms used is assumed. The context of his arguments
with Russell, Meinong, Stout, and many others would take a great
deal of study to reconstruct. But, basically, Eliot is interested in addressing the subject/object problem, and if the thesis is read in this
light, some of the technical difficulties can be seen as incidental, if
frustrating. The second and more profound difficulty lies in the nature of his claims which, to quote Gadamer's phrase about Heidegger, "constitute a thinking of nothingness repugnant to metaphysics" (TM, 228). There is a certain "unthinkable" quality about many
of Eliot's arguments, because of their circularity and lack of
grounding in an absolute of any kind.

Eliot's position is more radically modern than Bradley's because
of Eliot's more thorough refusal of subjectivity and acceptance of
hermeneutic foundations. Possibly critics turn to Bradley from this

---

12. Bolgan, *What the Thunder Really Said,* 181.

thesis because they are unwilling to think in Eliot's radical terms. Eliot is, I admit, still very much bound by Bradley's language and thus bound to a metaphysics which partly disallows his claims. Eliot never had a thorough critique of language (or of time) which would have freed him from the bounds of Bradley's idealism.

In light of Heidegger, Eliot's thesis emerges as a forceful presentation of an ontology which has no foundation other than finite existence. We should not be misled by the title of the published book, which seems to suggest an epistemological bias. Eliot quite forcefully rejects epistemology, devoting two out of six chapters in the thesis to this rejection. The 1964 title is an amendment of the original title, "Experience and the Objects of Knowledge in the Philosophy of F. H. Bradley," which more truly indicates Eliot's ontological concerns throughout the work. The problem of knowledge is an illusory one for Eliot. Instead, he is concerned with the status of those objects which we know, and their relation to a "larger" reality called experience.

Because of effective history, we are now able to see how far Eliot diverges in his thesis from Bradley's idealism. Bradley, of course, provides the basis for Eliot's thought, but the thesis is by no means a mere presentation of Bradley. Bradley is a very odd idealist in that his skepticism threatens to undermine idealism altogether. Yet, he remains an idealist at precisely the point where Eliot rejects him.

Richard Wollheim explains that, "In traditional Idealist thought . . . the existence of Things, Time, Space, Cause, is denied only to make the world a freer place for Self and God. In Bradley, however, the arguments that are used to dispossess material phenomena of reality are then turned against the phenomena of the spirit; the Self and God follow physical existences into the limbo of appearance."[13] The only reality is what Bradley calls "immediate experience," something prior to subject and object and clearly physical as much as mental, though he would deny the reality of these categories or any mental categories. Bradley's attitude toward the self is particularly interesting: "this wretched fraction and poor atom,

13. Richard Wollheim, *F. H. Bradley* (Baltimore, 1969), 220.

too mean to be in danger—do you mean to tell me that this bare remnant is really the self? the supposition is preposterous."[14]

Bradley also rejects any kind of transcendence in a universal mind or spirit. Reality is finite experience. But we cannot know experience; we can only know appearances. How do we then ever know reality and truth? Bradley's answer to this epistemological problem makes his metaphysics idealist. Bradley has a "formal criterion of truth"[15] by which truth (and reality) is non-contradictory: "Ultimate reality is such that it does not contradict itself; here is an absolute criterion" (AR, 136). Bradley postulates an Absolute which is the comprehensive and consistent unity of all experience, and which we approach through logical (consistent and coherent) ideas. These ideas are not innate, nor subjective; it is unclear how ideas come to be from an unknowable experience, which only appears as fragmentary and inconsistent. Through logical ideas, an order or form can be imposed on contradictory appearances in order to attain a non-subjective truth. Bradley wants this order to be somehow related to the unity of immediate experience, but, for Eliot, this order only participates in the idea of an Absolute, which can have nothing to do with the "here and now" of immediacy. Eliot makes this criticism of Bradley clear in an essay on Bradley and Leibniz written in 1916:

> Just as Leibniz' pluralism is ultimately based on faith, so Bradley's universe, actual only in finite centres, is only by an act of faith unified. Upon inspection, it falls away into the isolated finite experiences out of which it is put together. Like monads they aim at being one; each expanded to completion, to the full reality latent within it, would be identical with the whole universe. But in doing so it would lose the actuality, the here and now, which is essential to the small reality which it actually achieves. The Absolute responds only to an imaginary demand of thought, and satisfies only

14. F. H. Bradley, *Appearance and Reality* (2nd ed.; London, 1925), 81. Hereinafter cited parenthetically in the text as AR.
15. Allan, *Impersonal Theory*, 34.

> an imaginary demand of feeling. Pretending to be some-
> thing which makes finite centres cohere, it turns out to be
> merely the assertion that they do. And this assertion is only
> true so far as we here and now find it to be so.
>
> It is as difficult for Bradley as for Leibniz to maintain that
> there is any world at all. (KE, 202)

I quote at length here to suggest how thoroughly Eliot rejected the
idea of the Absolute and logical form at this point in his life. Several critics, working back from *Four Quartets* ("Only by the form,
the pattern/Can words or music reach/The stillness"), assert that
Eliot accepted this part of Bradley and that Bradley's idea of form
explains Eliot's Impersonal theory of poetry.[16] But a new reading of
his thesis proves this not to be so. Eliot maintains Bradley's skepticism about the self but joins it with a very modern existentialism
and non-subjective pragmatism, all of which set in motion a spin-
ning hermeneutic.

III

Eliot begins his thesis by presenting Bradley's idea
of "immediate experience" which is whole—both subject and object—and real. This "immediate experience" occurs in a "finite
center" which is a physical world, but is by no means a subject, because it is prior to the definition of self over against world:

> We must be on guard, in the first place, against identifying
> experience with consciousness, or against considering ex-
> perience as the adjective of a subject. We must not confuse
> immediate experience with sensation, we must not think of
> it as a sort of panorama passing before a reviewer, and we
> must avoid thinking of it as the content or substance of a
> mind. (KE, 15)

16. See Bolgan, *What the Thunder Really Said*, and Allan, *Impersonal Theory*.

Immediate experience, as reality, is absolutely finite and non-subjective. And, as reality, immediate experience is the "starting point of knowledge" (KE, 15). But this experience is not prior to knowledge nor in any way ever separate from knowledge. Nor is it available to knowledge as immediate experience; for knowledge to exist, relations and distinctions, particularly that between a knower and a known, must exist. These relations are constructed (ideal) from reality:

> But we go on to find that no actual experience could be merely immediate, for if it were, we should certainly know nothing about it; and also that the line between the experienced, or the given, and the constructed can nowhere be clearly drawn. Then we discover that the difference in no instance holds good outside of a relative and fluctuating point of view. Experience alone is real, but every*thing* can be experienced. And although immediate experience is the foundation and the goal of our knowing, yet no experience is only immediate. There is no absolute point of view from which real and ideal can be finally separated and labelled. (KE, 18)

The hermeneutic nature of these claims is clear. Immediate experience is foundational for knowledge but insofar as this foundation can be said to exist, it is known, and thus is no longer immediate experience. Experience (the real) and knowledge (the ideal) ground each other at every point. Reality both escapes and determines our constructions, but without our constructions no*thing* could be said to exist.

How do we know that there is any reality other than what we know? "The real, we are told, is felt," and this feeling is according to Bradley "a sort of confusion" (KE, 19). Eliot explains that this feeling is not subjective but is a sense of the unity of subject and object; however, insofar as we are aware of this feeling it cannot be immediate experience because we are aware of it only as a particular emotion or thought, that is, as something objectified. This special sense of feeling forms a link between experience and knowledge, and for this reason Eliot says that "feeling is self-transcendent" (KE, 21). While the feeling *is* the object of feeling, there is also something that escapes, is "not consistent" in Bradley's terms (KE, 28). This explanation seems insufficient and I will return to it later.

All distinctions and relations are abstractions from immediate experience, but without relations nothing could be known (without things no things could be known). Subject and object define each other as aspects of reality; though ideal constructions, they are yet real in Eliot's system. In his examination of the distinction between "ideal" and "real" in chapter 2, Eliot's thoughts begin to diverge from Bradley's in a radical way. Eliot defines the ideal in such a way as to make it always infused with the real, while Eliot asserts that Bradley defines ideas as either subjective or logical, neither of which is real in the sense of immediate experience. Eliot says that, "Both Bradley and Moore make but one distinction—that between a *psychical* idea and a *logical* idea" (KE, 41). But for Eliot the idea is neither psychical nor logical; he believes that Bradley has confused universal concepts (like redness or triangularity) with ideas.

For Bradley, the idea seems to attain to logical meaning so that ideas may avoid the inconsistency of the finite world and mirror Absolute reality. Bradley says, "For logical purposes ideas are symbols" (KE, 47), and, further, he defines the symbol as a sign with existence apart from its content, as a fox is a symbol for cunning. Eliot is troubled by this definition: "And here I find serious difficulties with Mr. Bradley's views. . . . Such a view would surely lead us to a representational theory of knowledge" (KE, 47–48). For Eliot, Bradley's definition of idea severs knowledge from actual finite existence, which is the only foundation for truth.

Eliot's argument against Bradley is difficult to paraphrase because he is trying to redefine the ideas of "idea" within the bounds of idealist thinking: "Should I apologize," he asks in a footnote, "for the fact that my use of 'idea' does not correspond with that of any author with whom I am acquainted?" (KE, 56). For him:

> The idea is the total content which we mean about reality
> in any particular presentation. It is not purely or even pri-

> marily psychological, for its meaning is essential (and meaning, as I shall have occasion to consider later, does not as such form an object for psychology); and furthermore, its meaning partially coincides with the reality which it intends. Nor is the idea purely a logical entity, since it always, in the end, comes to occupy a particular place in a real world. (KE, 40)

The idea is *always* connected to finite existence and as such the idea is changing and contextual, neither logical nor subjective. Through the idea, reality becomes a meaningful world. Reality and world are *of* each other through the idea:

> Ideas as I have claimed are not objects, but occupy a halfway stage between existence and meaning. ... Another person, and in its degree, another *thing*, is not for us simply an object; there is always, I believe, a felt continuity between the object and oneself. The only error lies in regarding this community as due to the common possession of a character which belongs to both subject and object as such, and belongs to each independently. This character is then treated as a thing. (KE, 80–81)

Eliot sees Bradley as abstracting the continuity between the object and oneself and treating it as a thing of logic. But for Eliot the idea is the continuity between existence and meaning for us, both of which are dependent on the other. This dependence, this act of interpreting reality as meaningful, is *idea* for Eliot:

> We have seen that the word "idea" does not refer to something ("thing") which intervenes between the object and the percipient, but is a stage in the process of realization of a world. The object so far as there is an object is presented to the knower without mediation of category or other psychological apparatus. ... knowledge is not a relation. The real world is not inside or outside ... it simply is. (KE, 138–139)

An important feature of Eliot's "idea" is that it is never given in a single word, for "only in the sentence does the word first acquire actual life and being" (KE, 38). That is, the idea is contextual, part of a world system of meaning, just as the semantic value of a word is dependent on its context: "The idea, from one point of view apart from the world and attached to it, yet contains already the character of the world, a world, as I said before, which shows by the very fact that idea can be attached to it that it is somehow prepared for the reception of that idea" (KE, 39). Again, we can see the hermeneutic character of Eliot's thought. The idea is not grafted on to a separate reality. Rather, in order for an idea to have meaning, it must arise out of a world (notice Eliot's indefinite article) even as it defines the world. Ideas are dependent on their world context, as the world is dependent on the idea. This idea of world is a key to Eliot's thought, as it is to Heidegger's.

For Eliot, the ideal cannot be defined without including the real. For while "experience alone is real," "no experience is only immediate" (KE, 18). Instead, we experience things—which are idealizations: "everything can be experienced." Therefore, "there is no absolute point of view from which real and ideal can be finally separated and labelled" (KE, 18). But because "real" and "ideal" are ideas abstracted from immediate experience, it does not follow that we are in a totally ideal world completely cut off from true reality. Ideas are real: "So far as the idea is real . . . it is not idea; and so far as it is not real it is not idea. This is equally true of ideas of imagination or of ideas of memory" (KE, 75). Ideas and reality are never two different groups of objects, nor even a process and an object; they are one process: "Reality is simply that which is intended and the ideal is that which intends" (KE, 36). The language of phenomenology is no accident here, for Eliot elsewhere expresses interest in the noetic act. Although Husserl is never mentioned in the thesis, Eliot does spend a good deal of time discussing the work of Alexius Meinong, who studied under the ur-phenomenologist Franz Brentano at roughly the same time as Husserl. Eliot says that he agrees with Meinong that consciousness is never a thing in itself, but is always consciousness of something. But Eliot disagrees with Meinong's division of objects into real and ideal categories: *inferiora* (mere being) and *superiora* (qualities and meanings) (KE, 95). Meinong's theories are evidently very complex, and Eliot interprets him with "great trepidation" (KE, 95). Still, when Meinong asserts the independence of qualities from being, Eliot acuses him of being a critical philosopher in the Kantian mode. To Eliot it is a senseless statement that we can grasp things apart from qualities and relations, which alone are available to consciousness, or that we can grasp qualities apart from finite things (KE, 97).

Though Eliot is attracted to the phenomenological method of rejecting assumptions about reality in order to describe the world accurately, he would necessarily reject Husserl's "transcendental ego" (as Heidegger did), as he rejects Meinong's categories and Bradley's logical ideas as ways to reach an Absolute. For Eliot, the object exists only insofar as it has meaning (ideality) for us in our world, but it is nonetheless real for that:

> What we are conscious of is *object* . . . an object which is conditioned by our knowledge of it because it is *our* object; but which is real and not mere *Erscheinung* (appearance)— which is, *qua* our object, independent of us. The sensation is at once a *Bestimmung* (determination) of the object and of the *Ich* (the self). . . . The *Ich* and its objects then form metaphysically one whole. (KE, 71)

Again and again Eliot stresses the seeming paradox that both the subject and object are ideal constructions and yet also real. Eliot explains that everything that is is a "point of attention" in which the thing becomes objectified (with ideas) and thus comes into existence as a thing. Eliot understands the difficulty of this hermeneutic:

> It is only as the point of attention becomes qualified—becomes a *what*—that it is even a *that*; a number of characteristics, none of which is essential to its objectivity, and none of which is objective in the sense of being an object, nevertheless constitute *its* objectivity: its *thatness* is in direct ratio to its *whatness*. And the thing, in order to be a thing even,

> must be capable of entering into a kind of existence in which
> it is not a thing. I do not argue that a thing ceases to be a
> thing when it ceases to be a point of attention: this is I be-
> lieve supposed to be the point of view of subjective ideal-
> ism. . . . The thing does not cease to exist, it exists in other
> ways, ways which are not thinghood, but can only be ex-
> pressed in terms of thinghood. And without the potential-
> ity of these other forms of existence the thing would not
> even be a thing: *existence, I mean to say, is not identical with
> thinghood.* . . . The account which I offer is, I know, any-
> thing but lucid! (KE, 99–100)

That something is (reality, its Being) and *what* something is (ideality, a being) are hermeneutically founded upon each other. Though
the reality of immediate experience (that things are) is always hid-
den from us, this reality does come to light as whatness, as things.
But the thing, those qualities which we know, never adequately expresses its existence, which remains concealed. And because "existence is not identical with thinghood," there is potential for other
forms and other interpretations of the thing. The potential is the
existence within a thing by which it is a thing and by which it may
change through time.

Eliot is not overly worried about this indeterminacy. "What constitutes a real object," he writes, "is the practical need or occasion"
(KE, 101). Eliot supports a practical approach to metaphysics when-
ever possible: "the real world of practice is essentially vague, un-
precise, swarming with what are, from a metaphysical point of view,
insoluble contradictions. . . . This world is what it is by reason of
the practical point of view" (KE, 136). The world shapes itself to our
needs. And though Eliot never develops this connection, there is
inevitably a connection between the feeling of "confusion" which
constitutes our awareness of immediate experience (see above), our
needs as finite beings, and the continuing constitution of the world.
My interpretation is admittedly Heideggerian, but the elements are
all there in Eliot. Our immediate experience (thrownness), revealed
in a feeling of confusion (anxiety), is gathered up in ideas (projec-

tion) by which we determine and recognize the things which we need (concern).

The structure is "world-time" for Heidegger, not the "sequence of 'nows'" which is the scientific approach to time.[17] Eliot is concerned about time in his thesis, wondering what "persists in time" (KE, 101) given the indeterminacy of things. For him, time is a succession of nows, and he concludes that only a pure *that* (which is impossible) would be wholly in time, because ideas as relations and meanings very specifically counter the succession of nows. Eliot remains practical here: "Ordinarily there is no difficulty [about what persists in time], for the object is not *bestimmt*: it fluctuates as occasion demands . . . but as the terms are analyzed into relations, it appears finally that nothing is in time except time itself" (KE, 101–102). Eliot's willingness to push his analysis to this limit reveals his understanding of the inadequacy of thinking of time as a succession of nows. Earlier in the thesis, he interprets time quite differently: "The present of ideal construction, the present of meaning and not simply of psychical or physical process, is really a span which includes my present ideas of past and future" (KE, 55). The "present of meaning," which includes future and past, is an alternative to an empty now, though Eliot never develops this idea.

The pragmatic streak in this book is not to be confused with the pragmatism of William James, which Eliot rejects for its subjectivity. Eliot's pragmatism is not of the self but of a world in which subjects and objects are determined systemically as experience demands. Eliot's brief discussion of language and the relation between words, objects, and meaning is relevant to this non-subjective pragmatism. There is a hermeneutic relationship between the diacritical system, by which meanings change and grow in a system of differences, and the word, which is attached to reality.

"Without words, no objects," Eliot declares (KE, 132). But he ex-

---

17. Heidegger, *Being and Time*, 474: "*Significance* belongs to the structure of the 'now.' We have accordingly called the time with which we concern ourselves '*world*-time.' In the ordinary interpretations of time as a sequence of 'nows,' both datability and significance are *missing*." Eliot also distinguishes ordinary time from the "present of meaning" (KE, 55).

plains, "I am very far from meaning that it is the act of naming which makes the object, for the activity does not proceed from one side more than from another. Objects cannot arise without names, and names never spring up without objects. . . . Nor do I mean that the object did not exist until it was known, but only that it has not the character of objectivity until it is known as an object" (KE, 133–34). Still: "The name is not the object. . . . It denotes an object which is not itself, and yet, when we ask just what this object is which is denoted, we have nothing to point to but the name . . . we denote not its *whatness* but its *thatness*" (KE, 134). The interrelatedness of *whatness* (objectivity as a being) and *thatness* (existence or Being) is absolute for Eliot. The word is the reality, the concept of the object, but it is not the objectness of the object. In Bradley's example, sugar is white, sweet, and hard but it is not merely these qualities. Sugar *is*. The name denotes *thatness* but its meaning is its *whatness*: "the word (here the existent) is continuous with the meaning (here subsistent)" (KE, 104). The meaning comes only from a context or sentence in which relations are specified. The sentence is the idea, and ideas, the meaningful relations between objects, are the world. The relational (meaning, world) and the existential (concept, reality) are *always* found together. The word refers to/creates a reality, but it also has meaning only in a system.

Paul Ricoeur finds this "tension" in language exemplified in the copula "is," which is both predicative ("sugar is sweet") and existential ("sugar is"). The existential force of "is" (the denotation of *thatness* for Eliot) remains present even in its predicative function (as *whatness*), such that an "is not" is exposed within the "is." The statement "sugar is sweet" has within it "sugar is not sweet but is sugar" or "sugar is not sugar, but is sweet." For Ricoeur, this affirming/denying structure of "is" is the key to the polysemy and metaphoricity of language. "Is" both affirms and denies equivalence. At the level of the word, the word is the reality, but *is not* the reality. At the clearer level of the metaphor the maiden's cheeks both are and are not roses. For a rose is a rose; no other qualities denote it. But, we know the rose as red and soft and velvety like the cheeks of the maiden that are denoted only by "cheeks," but *mean* red and soft and velvety. The deep "is not" in a word keeps it both autonomous—free to change meaning in its own diacritical system as the object changes meaning in the practical context of a world—and denotative of a reality. The word, like the object, participates in the real, *because of* the absence of permanent definition.[18]

The human is necessary for this hermeneutic of language and world, but the event of meaning does not happen in a psyche. In this context we can see how thoroughly Eliot rejects Bradley's incipient subjectivism, even solipsism. Although Eliot learned his skepticism about the self from Bradley, he accuses Bradley of a certain amount of subjectivism in discussing ideas. Eliot quotes Bradley as saying that "the idea . . . is assuredly a psychical event . . . A truth, we may say, is no truth at all unless it happens in a soul" (KE, 77).[19] This is a grave confusion of psychology and metaphysics for Eliot: "A truth as such is quite independent of finite soul, and we may say that it is the finitude of truth which constitutes the finite soul" (KE, 77–78). This statement is open to some interpretation since "truth" is never clearly defined by Eliot. But it appears that truth is nonsubjective and finite—seemingly a double rejection of idealism. And in a typical hermeneutic reversal, Eliot lays man's finitude to the finitude of truth which destroys the possibility of an absolute. There is for Eliot no mental content apart from the external "real" world (KE, 83). He specifically rejects Bradley's statement that the subject has certain qualities or dispositions:

> Now I question whether it is ever a "psychical" fact which we take as the subject in a disposition. Men are avaricious, generous, vicious, or self-sacrificing, and these qualities I suppose are dispositions. But avarice and generosity are not psychical events but social interpretations of behavior, behavior involving the whole organism. What is in the mind of the avaricious or generous man is not avarice or generosity, but a real world qualified in a certain way. (KE, 79)

18. Ricoeur, *Rule of Metaphor*, 247–56.
19. Soul, for Bradley, is neither spirit nor self, but a "finite centre" to which he gives psychological qualities. AR, 298.

Mowbray Allan interprets statements like this one as showing Eliot's position to be midway between subjective idealism and behaviorism, though he does not define what this position might be.[20] The introduction of behaviorism into the discussion is as misleading as continuing to think in terms of idealism, for Eliot rejected the purely physical as thoroughly as the purely mental. The human is always absolutely attached to its physical world, but the world is a human one, shaped by emotions and ideas. Thus, "the emotion is really part of the object, and is ultimately just as objective. Hence when the object, or complex of objects, is recalled, the pleasure is recalled in the same way, and is naturally recalled on the object side rather than the subject side" (KE, 80). We all know how Eliot the critic used this philosophical insight in the formulation of the "objective correlative" (see Chapter Four).

Eliot develops his alternative to Bradley's idealism throughout the thesis, even though in the conclusion he writes, "I believe that all of the conclusions that I have reached are in substantial agreement with *Appearance and Reality*, though I have been compelled to reject certain theories, logical and psychological, which appear in the *Principles* and elsewhere" (KE, 153). And, indeed, Eliot's argument with psychology in chapter 3 against the reality of internal mental states and his argument with epistemology in chapters 4 and 5 against the existence of an external reality independent of man are developments from Bradley's theories, though, in my opinion, much more significant developments than critics have been willing to admit. Eliot is drawn to the lack of essences in Bradley's metaphysics, but is not at all interested in a logical Absolute as foundational for truth. Nowhere in the thesis does Eliot suggest that ultimate truth is anything but the finitude of existence, which, manifest as world (meaning), is totally open to us, but, as reality (existence), is totally concealed from us: "We find that we are certain of everything—relatively, and of nothing—positively" (KE, 157). His rather forceful conclusion is that, "Any assertion about the *world*, or any *ultimate* statement about any *object in* the world, will inevitably be an

20. Allan, *Impersonal Theory*, 31–32.

interpretation" (KE, 165); therefore, philosophy "can ultimately be founded on nothing but faith" (KE, 163).

"Faith" is not incompatible with Eliot's insistence on finitude. When Bradley turns to an Absolute in order to escape the solipsism implicit in his idealism, Eliot's rejection is firm. He shows himself to be a good phenomenologist in replying to Bradley's claim that "for rejecting a higher experience [the Absolute] in which the appearances are transformed, I can find no reason."[21] Eliot replies: "But what we do know is that we are able to pass from one point of view to another, that we are compelled to do so, and that the different aspects more or less hang together. For rejecting a higher experience there may be no reason. But that this higher experience explains the lower is at least open to doubt" (KE, 207).

Eliot sees that Bradley needs the "higher experience" to escape the solipsism inherent in his separation of appearance from reality. Though Eliot made Bradley's extreme statement of solipsism famous when he quoted it in the notes to *The Waste Land*,[22] Eliot is no solipsist. Immediate experience is private in the sense that it is unknowable to others, but it is also unknowable to the self, since the self is as much an ideal construction as other selves: "And a doctrine of solipsism would have to show that my self and my states were immediately given, and other selves inferred. But just because what is given is not my self but my world, the question is meaningless" (KE, 150). "To realize that a point of view is a point of view is already to have transcended it" (KE, 148). That is, the realization of the self is always already an understanding of the world in which there are many others.[23] Why this is so, Eliot does not attempt to understand: "The process of the genesis of the self and of other selves

---

21. Quoted by Eliot, KE, 207, from F. H. Bradley, *Essays on Truth and Reality* (Oxford, 1914), 613.

22. "My external sensations are no less private to myself than are my thoughts or my feelings. In either case my experience falls within my own circle, a circle closed on the outside; and, with all its elements alike, every sphere is opaque to the others which surround it. . . . In brief, regarded as an existence which appears in a soul, the whole world is peculiar and private to that soul" (AR, 346).

23. As Jacques Lacan will show us (Chapter Five), you cannot have one until you have two.

is ultimately perhaps unknowable, since there is no 'because' which we can assign" (KE, 150–51). That we are in a meaningful world, that we cannot be isolated selves—that we are *Dasein*—these are givens.

The only foundation which we have is immediate experience, which, as concealed, is no foundation at all for metaphysics. Metaphysics can, then, only be founded on faith and will be rejected by conflicts with the practical world:

> The [metaphysician] thinks of reality in terms of his system; the [critic] thinks of the system in terms of the indefinite social reality. There occurs, in short, just what is sure to occur in a world in which subject and predicate are not one. Metaphysical systems are condemned to go up like a rocket and come down like a stick. (KE, 167–68)

Eliot does not seem to despair at this continual destruction. Our deep bond with the mystery of the real, which keeps us ever in an unfinished state of possibility, can be interpreted as an existential impulse toward creativity. Eliot the poet leaves behind just those elements in Bradley which deny this insight, in particular our separation from the real except in the form of an Absolute.

Bradley posits his Absolute on no more absolute a basis than that it satisfies the human need for harmony and wholeness. But for Eliot, this secular Absolute denies our experience:

> We are forced to the assumption that truth is one, and to the assumption that reality is one. But dissension arises when we ask the question: what one? . . . the world, as we have seen, exists only as it is found in the experiences of finite centres, experiences so mad and strange that they will be boiled away before you boil them down to one homogeneous mass. (KE, 168)

Eliot has a poet's fascination with the particularity of the world which is never illuminated in universals; his need for an Absolute can be satisfied only in something otherworldly. In this world, appearance and reality merge, so that only the teeming here and now is left, bounded by no absolutes:

> And if anyone assert that immediate experience, at either
> the beginning or end of our journey, is annihilation and ut-
> ter night, I cordially agree. That Mr. Bradley himself would
> accept this interpretation of his (*Truth and Reality*, p. 188)
> "positive, non-distinguished non-relational whole" is not
> to be presumed. (KE, 31)

This is the Eliot of *The Waste Land* and modernism speaking, and
his differences with Bradley should not be overlooked. Bradley's
skepticism remains a secular Victorian idealism, in which we know
nothing but appearances, even though through logic we can approach reality. But Eliot asserts that we know everything and nothing, because the distinction between appearance and reality cannot
be maintained. Finite existence is all there is—completely unknown to us in its essence and completely known to us in our practical lives, our world. The philosophy expressed in *Knowledge and
Experience* is deeply existential, denying the knowledge of any essence, but affirming meaning in spite of the lack of traditional
foundations. This affirmation results from Eliot's thoroughgoing
non-subjectivity, which aligns him not with the existential despair
of those who posit a meaningful subject in a meaningless world, but
with the hermeneutic existentialism of Heidegger.

The parallels with Heidegger's hermeneutics are clear. Consciousness and ideas are of a world, not of a subject (being-in-
the-world); the world, and therefore consciousness, is a state of
meaningful interpretations, neither ideal nor real; reality (Being) is
unknowable except as it comes to be interpreted as an ideal thing
(being); the absence of reality as a whole, coherent absolute (or rather
the presence of reality as absence, temporal change, and finitude)
keeps interpretative possibilities virtually limitless; future possibilities, past meanings, and present needs are intertwined and inseparable; and the things of the world include linguistic, imaginary, and affective things as ontologically equal to physical things;
all are interpretations.

Chapter Four

Criticism and
the Idea of World

The real world is neither inside nor outside—it simply is.

T. S. Eliot

Knowledge and Experience

I

My reading of Eliot's dissertation is, of course, an interpretation of the past from present concerns, as are all interpretations according to the principle of effective history. But the impossibility of knowing the past as past and the necessity of knowing past as present were not learned from continental criticism. It was Eliot himself who wrote in his most famous essay:

> But the difference between the present and the past is that the conscious present is an awareness of the past in a way and to an extent which the past's awareness of itself cannot show.
>
> Some one said: "The dead writers are remote from us because we *know* so much more than they did." Precisely, and they are that which we know.[1]

As I hope to show, that astonishing essay "Tradition and the Indi-

---

1. T.S. Eliot, "Tradition and Individual Talent," in *Selected Essays*, 6. This book will hereinafter be cited parenthetically in the text as SE.

vidual Talent," which seems to anticipate so much contemporary criticism, along with Eliot's other influential early essays, are not a chance collection of occasional remarks, but are a clear application of hermeneutic thinking to literary theory. Unfortunately, the first principles of Eliot's hermeneutics, particularly the rejection of subject/object dualism, could not have been understood by most readers of Eliot until recently, when what we know is no longer what Eliot knew (nineteenth-century idealism), but is Eliot himself (twentieth-century existentialism).

Those early critics of Eliot, who have so greatly influenced subsequent thought about his work, were certainly schooled in the same metaphysics Eliot was trying to dissect. But even later critics, who were nursed on twentieth-century philosophy (though still probably dualist philosophy), such as Hugh Kenner and Frank Kermode, have not yet absorbed Eliot as a thinker. Not finding any rational or logical system in Eliot's criticism, these critics deny Eliot's philosophical cast of mind altogether except as a rather vague interest in Bradley. For Kenner, Eliot had a "generalizing style" which was "brought to fruition . . . under the auspices of an idealist philosphy." Kermode 's outlook is that Eliot's theories are "highly personal versions of stock themes in the history of ideas of the period."[2]

This dismissive tendency has been countered by several recent studies which try to unify Eliot's thought. John Margolis, concentrating on Eliot's non-literary essays, particularly those in the *Criterion*, has found a coherent pattern of development based on Eliot's conviction that man must "do inner obeisance to something higher than his ordinary self." In spite of the diversity of Eliot's interests, Margolis shows how Eliot's on-going argument with romanticism, his social and political views, and his religious conversion all spring from the same source, that is, the search for an external authority to make up for "the insufficiency of the autonomous individual."[3]

---

2. Kenner, *Invisible Poet*, 42–43; Frank Kermode, "A Babylonish Dialect," *Sewanee Review*, LXXIV (1966), 230.
3. Margolis, *T.S. Eliot's Intellectual Development*, 8, 26.

The non-literary essays reveal that Eliot's classicism and conservatism are rooted in doubt about the self and not in the dogmatic self-assertion evident in his teacher and mentor Irving Babbitt. Eliot understands the connection between dogmatism and individualism, and criticizes those like Babbitt who deny "the mob part of the mind in themselves" (SE, 422). For Eliot, Babbitt does not have a sufficient historical awareness, and thus Babbitt has an inappropriate faith in his own reason:

> The great men whom he holds up for our admiration and example are torn from their contexts of race, place, and time. And in consequence, Mr. Babbitt seems to me to tear himself from his own context. . . . But the historical humanist, as I understand him, halts at a certain point and admits that the reason will go no farther. (SE, 422–23)

Eliot's critique of the self is not a result of either religious or political beliefs, but of a complex philosophical awareness of the effect of finitude and historical change on our assumptions about subjectivity and objectivity. Because Margolis does not deal with the dissertation at all, his book is limited only to describing Eliot's nonliterary thought and offers no analysis of the philosophical cast of mind behind Eliot's tolerant conservatism. Still, Eliot's critique of the self, emphasized by Margolis, is central in all of Eliot's thought, most strikingly in his literary theory.

Lewis Freed in his book *T. S. Eliot: The Critic as Philosopher* has thoroughly documented the refusal by critics to take Eliot seriously as a thinker.[4] Freed's book is an admirable attempt to study Eliot's criticism in light of the dissertation. But this book, like so many other efforts to address Eliot's ideas, misinterprets by relying too heavily on Bradley and on Cartesian assumptions about the self. For example, Freed quotes Eliot's criticism of Matthew Arnold for misusing words, specifically for using the words *truth* and *thing* as interchangeable. Freed explains Eliot's position by quoting Aristotle to the effect that "falsity and truth are not in things . . . but in

4. Freed, *Critic as Philosopher*, Chaps. 1 and 2.

thought," and quoting Bradley regarding "the distinction between things and my thoughts about them." Freed goes on to emphasize the connection of truth with thought for Eliot.[5] I would not wish to speak for Aristotle or Bradley, but the Eliot of *Knowledge and Experience* very firmly rejects the idealist basis for the connection of truth and thought as opposed to things. Rather, thought and things belong together as interpretation; wherever truth lies, it is not in subjective thought. Freed is stumbling over Eliot's denial of the primacy of human consciousness; Eliot's definition of idea does not distinguish between the thing and our ideas about the thing. Freed, like many others, indiscriminately quotes from Bradley and Eliot together, usually using Bradley's more traditional idealism to clarify Eliot's difficult and radical thought and to bolster the critic's own convictions about the self.

For these reasons, "Tradition and the Individual Talent" and the other early essays have yet to be given their due as statements as new as Eliot's poetry was new. Eliot's ideas of tradition and the impersonal are often taken as standing for some timeless, universal "still point" in opposition to the particular and temporal individual. But tradition for Eliot is precisely change and novelty; and the impersonal requires an individual and particular view of the object. Those critics who understand this complexity still tend to explain these concepts by reference to "form" defined in terms of Bradley's consistent and complete Absolute. I do not believe that Eliot's idea of form is adequately (or even accurately) described by a discussion of idealist logic, Hegelian organic form, or a coherence theory of truth.[6] But form is a word which Eliot does equate with both tradition and the impersonal. Keeping in mind Eliot's non-subjective and non-essential cast of mind, let us see what these terms could

5. *Ibid.*, 16.
6. Freed, *Critic as Philosopher*, in his last chapter uses idealist logic to explain Eliot's idea of form, while Allan, *Impersonal Theory*, 146–50, compares Eliot's "form" to a coherence theory of truth. I have already advanced arguments against an idealist interpretation of Eliot. Eliot himself addresses the coherence theory of truth at the end of *Knowledge and Experience*: "For what is it that coheres? ideas, we shall be told, and not realities; and the whole structure is a faquir's show for a penny" (KE, 168).

mean for Eliot and how they are manifested in his practical criticism.

II

In *After Strange Gods* (1934) Eliot writes that we are not "to associate tradition with the immovable; to think of it as something hostile to all change," for "the word itself implies a movement."[7] Earlier, in 1921, Eliot associates novelty with tradition, and staleness with lack of tradition: "Culture is traditional and loves novelty; the General Reading Public knows no tradition and loves staleness."[8] As Eliot knows, these definitions run counter to the ordinary use of the word *traditional*, which would never be applied to Eliot's own poetry, for instance. Eliot's idea of tradition is actually a theory of aesthetic history, or historical aesthetics; for Eliot, history and aesthetics cannot be properly separated. The truly artistic is absolutely in its own time; being of its own time requires novelty, but being of a time is also being of history. The now must conform to the history it belongs to, as history conforms to and changes to include the now. In "Tradition and the Individual Talent" Eliot writes:

> The necessity that he [the poet] shall conform, that he shall cohere, is not onesided; what happens when a new work of art is created is something that happens simultaneously to all the works of art which preceded it. . . . Whoever has approved this idea of order, of the form of European, of English literature will not find it preposterous that the past should be altered by the present as much as the present is directed by the past. (SE, 5)

Eliot's simple statement of the principle of effective history does not mean to subjectivize history. These changes do not occur in our

7. T. S. Eliot, *After Strange Gods* (New York, 1934), 18, 23–24.
8. T. S. Eliot, "London Letter," *Dial*, LXX (1921), 451.

minds; the changes occur in the possibilities for meaning, that is, as *Knowledge and Experience* tells us, meaning is of a world, not of a self. Eliot's idea of world as a diacritical system of meaning is, in this essay, called "the mind of Europe," or broadly, tradition. World, we must remember, is never just physical, but is all "ideal" things: objects, ideas, art, illusions, selves—and, Eliot reminds us, the things of the past:

> [The poet] must be aware that the mind of Europe—the mind of his own country—a mind which he learns in time to be much more important than his own private mind—is a mind which changes, and that this change is a development which abandons nothing *en route*, which does not superannuate either Shakespeare, or Homer, or the rock drawing of the Magdalenian draughtsman. (SE, 6)

Eliot is careful not to identify this changing mind with any kind of Hegelian progress toward Spirit (or Bradleyan progress toward the Absolute): "This development, refinement perhaps, complication certainly, is not, from the point of view of the artist, any improvement" (SE, 6). The changes might even be "based upon a complication in economics and machinery" (SE, 6). In other words, Eliot speculates that historical change results from pragmatic concerns of our finite world and not from the call of some Ideal.

Change is not merely an aspect of tradition, but *is* tradition. Not only is novelty "better than repetition" (SE, 4), but, for a work of art, "To conform merely would be for the new work not really to conform at all; it would not be new, and would therefore not be a work of art" (SE, 5). A work of art is a new thing in the world, arising from a particular and unique time and place. Only in the newness does tradition exist, as history would not exist without the continual change of events guaranteed by the world's finitude and temporality. Being of a particular time ensures that the work of art will also be of the tradition, for the tradition constitutes the world of that time.

We are, of course, always of a particular world and, thus, of a tradition, "the mind of our country." But the poet, for Eliot, must be conscious of this situation: "[Tradition] cannot be inherited, and if you want it you must obtain it by great labour" (SE, 4). Eliot insists that the artist must obtain the "historical sense" which involves a perception "not only of the pastness of the past, but of its presence . . . it is at the same time what makes a writer most acutely conscious of his place in time, of his own contemporaneity" (SE, 4). The artist only gains this sense through education, though not necessarily an academic or systematic education: "Shakespeare acquired more essential history from Plutarch than most men could from the whole British Museum" (SE, 6). Formal education may obscure an individual's uniqueness; but one must have an "essential" knowledge of the identity and difference between one's own age and the past. The present and the past cannot ever be known apart from each other, for they hermeneutically define each other. Knowledge of the past is mostly knowledge of the point of view from which we see the past, while knowledge of one's point of view is mostly knowledge of the past which determines this point of view.

Now, the point of view, while in some sense *my* point of view, is not subjective or mental. It is impersonal: "The progress of an artist is a continual self-sacrifice, a continual extinction of personality" (SE, 7). The poem is not of the self but is of the tradition and the world. The poem is, for Eliot, an independent object, but also an object in a world—a qualification that some New Critics have not always heeded. The poet cannot be said to invent the poem except in the dual sense of invent: to create and discover. The active and conscious work of knowing the tradition must be coupled with a "passive attending upon the event" (SE, 10), which allows the poet's world (unique, but impersonal thanks to the study of tradition) to create. The conscious work does not make the poet's personality more poetic, it only releases him from a rigid subjectivity of vision and invites new realities to come to expression: "The mind of the mature poet differs from that of the immature one not precisely in any valuation of 'personality,' not being necessarily more interesting, or having 'more to say,' but rather by being a more finely perfected medium in which special, or very varied, feelings are at liberty to enter into new combinations" (SE, 7). Eliot's anti-romantic view is particularly emphasized by his famous scientific analogy: the poet's mind is a catalyst which allows two elements to combine and form a new substance containing no trace of the catalyst (SE, 7). This depersonalizing analogy has irritated some readers, like Stephen Spender, who writes, "This is probably the most pretentious and most questionable of his scientific analogies. The scientific model tends to distract from the poetic behavior it is supposed to describe and focuses the reader on the model itself."[9] It is exactly Eliot's purpose to remove the poet from any suggestion of subjective behavior. The impersonal is not a metaphor for a specialized poetic inner state. For Eliot, the self, the reification of mental states, only obscures the creative possibility of human being-in-the-world. The human is not thrown out with the self.

Eliot's concept of the impersonal has given other critics trouble, too, partly because of Eliot's seemingly contradictory statements about personality, and partly because of the assumptions about the self being brought to bear on Eliot's ideas. Eliot uses *impersonal* and *personality* in both negative and positive ways in his practical criticism. The impersonal can mean what is merely conventional, public, "at best, part of the public character; or at worst, catchwords" (KE, 165). Here the impersonal suggests the reification of convention into something which cannot change with the world. Eliot is not opposed to convention; in his dissertation he says, "Reality is a convention" (KE, 98). But the finite here and now is only grasped by constant change. In his essay on Blake (1920), Eliot rejects the public conformity which is often what the educational system imposes: "For these processes consist largely in the acquisition of impersonal ideas which obscure what we really are and feel, what we really want, and what really excites our interest" (SE, 277). Eliot's opposition to the uncritical acceptance of public ideas is balanced by his rejection of subjective states and emotions (though these, too, are actually social conventions in Eliot's eyes). In the dissertation, Eliot denies that there is any mental content at all in the form of a self or personality (KE, 83). What we call personality is merely a fragment of a larger whole, a fragment which, when taken

9. Stephen Spender, *T. S. Eliot* (New York, 1975), 72.

in isolation, is artifical and misleading. The isolation of the self from the world introduces the epistemological problem, resulting in either an overblown belief in the self (romantic individualism) or a crippling sense of the relativity of all knowledge (liberal humanism), neither of which had any validity for Eliot.

What is left, apart from the social and the personal, is what Eliot calls in his criticism "the impersonal" and in his thesis "point of view" (neither the static, ideal self, nor the real, but unknowable, immediate experience). It is characterized, rather paradoxically, by an intensely unique particularity which sheds public ideas, even those about the self, and sees freshly. As Eliot says admiringly of Blake: "He was naked, and saw man naked, and from the centre of his own crystal" (SE, 277). This particularity is our physical finitude, our unique point of view which is as obscured by ideas of the self as by ideas of the object. But this particularity is not the unattainable immediacy of experience. It is in a time and place that is a world. The hermeneutic idea of world is as important for understanding the impersonal as for understanding tradition. The world is the place of meaning, of relations, of interpretation, and of tradition. The world is the place of subject and object, although the reification of these constructions blinds us to their contextual dependence on a world and to the contextual dependence of all knowledge. The "historical sense" and the "impersonal" do not bring us a truth which is contextually independent; they make us aware that our world is not a place of essences and fixity, but is a place of interpretation and movement, neither caused by, nor centered upon, the reified self, but necessitated by finite human existence. The escape from the self, that "surrender" and "extinction" of personality (SE, 6–7), is not into something more universal than the "self," but into something more particular and finite, which is the place of the world.

Throughout his criticism, Eliot insists that the more particular a poet is, the more universal that poet is. Writing of Yeats in 1940, he says, "in becoming more Irish . . . he became at the same time universal."[10] I do not believe that Eliot wishes to imply the idealism

10. T. S. Eliot, *On Poetry and Poets* (New York, 1957), 301.

of "concrete universals"; it is significant that Eliot, unlike so many modernist critics, does not use this term, even though he was undoubtedly familiar with the arguments concerning concrete universals beginning with Hegel. For Bradley and other idealists, the only true concrete universal would be the Absolute, which includes all real and ideal things; generally, ideas which have universal meaning are always separated from the real and concrete experience. As we saw earlier, Eliot developed his own notion of idea as something participating in the object and in reality; therefore the concrete detail is the meaning and does not refer to or even express a meaning other than itself. The "holism" of a theory of concrete universals is often achieved by finding a logical structure or a new whole encompassing the details. John Crowe Ransom argued against this theory by claiming that poetry must have "irrelevant" details that won't fit into any logical whole.[11] Though this argument of Ransom's is virtually the same one that he leveled against Eliot's claim, in "The Metaphysical Poets," that "in the mind of the poet these [disparate] experiences are always forming new wholes" (SE, 247), Eliot is perhaps closer to Ransom than is generally thought. What could the poet of so fragmented a poem as *The Waste Land* mean by forming new wholes?

We are led back to Eliot's idea of world, which is a whole, but not a logical or fixed whole. The world is a diacritical whole, the relational structure formed by everything that is. A diacritical whole can mediate between the claims that the identity of the concrete detail is merged into a larger universal and the claims that the identity of the concrete can never be changed. As Ricoeur points out, these are the two poles of discussion about metaphoric truth: the pole of belief or "ontological naïveté" which sees the concrete as totally transformed into a new whole, and the pole of disbelief which sees the metaphoric process as a fiction which does not ontologically alter the identity of the concrete details. For Ricoeur, these

11. Ransom, *The New Criticism*, 280, 314. Ransom's criticism of Eliot's "wholes" is on pages 183–84. Ransom speaks of the "ontological density" of modern poetry, page 335.

poles correspond to the dual nature of the copula discussed earlier: "is" is both existential and relational. At the pole of belief, the metaphoric "is" is always existential, while at the pole of disbelief it is relational.[12] Ricoeur wishes to preserve the dual sense of the copula in metaphor, as I believe Eliot sees that the relational (whatness) is inseparable from the existential (thatness): "Its *thatness* is in direct ratio to its *whatness*" (KE, 99), writes Eliot of a thing ("thing" is Eliot's generic word for all ideas, objects, universals, and particulars [KE, 162–63]). The disparate things—in Eliot's example, falling in love, reading Spinoza, the noise of the typewriter, and the smell of cooking (SE, 247)—are not discrete entities or experiences but exist only by their relations or meaningful place in a world. The "that" and the "what" are absolutely related, but not the same. For when the meaningful relationships are drastically (and successfully) changed—as in a metaphor—so that falling in love and reading Spinosa are a new whole rather than peripherally related experiences, there is an ontological change in the world, in the relational whatness, but not in the thatness of the thing. A new thing comes into existence with the new meaning. And the reality of the particulars is not dimmed but is affirmed in their ability to change meaning—that ability is their concealing/revealing reality. For, "without the potentiality of these other forms of existence, the thing would not even be a thing" (KE, 100). Both the old and the new meaning must be held in tension in order to reveal the mystery of the particular: its "existence" (thatness), which we cannot know, "is not identical with thinghood" (whatness), the meaning which we know (KE, 100). And only through the particular is this truth seen, for it cannot be otherwise known. If the particular were capable of being totally transformed into a new whole, the moment of tension could not be seen, and if the particular were totally explained by its relation in a universal structure, then its ungraspable and excessive

12. Ricoeur, *Rule of Metaphor*, 247–56, refers to Philip Wheelwright, *The Burning Fountain* (Bloomington, 1968), and Colin Murray Turbayne, *The Myth of Metaphor* (New Haven, 1962), as examples of the poles of belief and disbelief respectively.

existence as a thing would be lost.[13] In other words, for Eliot, existence exceeds meaning; but in the concrete universal, meaning exceeds existence.

The poem should indeed not mean, but be; however, being requires meaning. But the business of the poet is not to create meaning. The meaning should inhere in the particulars because of their world both in and out of the poem. I believe that Eliot's criticisms of Blake are due to the completeness with which, for Eliot, Blake's long poems are severed from any world other than their own. The power of Blake's point of view allowed him to present "only the essential, only, in fact, what can be presented, and need not be explained" (se, 277). But when Blake seeks to explain, as in his long poems, Eliot says that "the form is not well chosen" (se, 278). The problem for Blake is that he must have meanings, but he is unsatisfied with the world and the tradition which hold meaning. Therefore, he creates his own world, a world complex and rich with internal relational meaning, but severed from external relational meaning. Eliot writes, "And about Blake's supernatural territories, as about the supposed ideas that dwell there, we cannot help commenting on a certain meanness of culture" (se, 279). This remarkable truth about Blake indicates Blake's power for the adventurous reader: the long poems attempt to make their own world, even while understanding that creation comes only from a world. The powerful hermeneutic truth embodied in these works, the naked vision of reality, is for Eliot obscured by Blake's need to explain a world, leaving him little time to present it.[14] For Eliot, the explanations

13. Ransom would call this "Platonic poetry," "which is really science but masquerades as poetry by affecting a concern for physical objects." *The World's Body* (New York, 1938), 121–22.

14. The hermeneutic circle in Blake is, I believe, central to Donald Ault's study of *The Four Zoas,* although his terminology is quite different from mine. Ault's illuminating argument reveals that *The Four Zoas* does present the process of a world creating itself (a world worlding in Heidegger's terms). The many difficulties of the poem stem from the fact that the poem presents the creation of a world which could only be created after that world exists. The world and the creation of that world are mutually dependent on each other. Blake's difficulty in *realizing* this complexity is manifest in the highly revised state of the manuscript of *The Four Zoas.* See Donald Ault, *Narrative Unbound: Re-visioning Blake's "Four Zoas",* forthcoming from Station Hill Press.

are unnecessary if the poet understands the world as it is and lets it do the work of meaning: "The weakness of the long poems is certainly not that they are too visionary. . . . Blake did not see enough, became too much occupied with ideas. . . . What his genius required, and what it sadly lacked, was a framework of accepted and traditional ideas which would have prevented him from indulging in a philosophy of his own, and concentrated his attention upon the problems of the poet" (SE, 278–80).

Eliot found Blake too *conscious* a poet. In "Tradition and the Individual Talent" he writes, "The bad poet is usually unconscious where he ought to be conscious, and conscious where he ought to be unconscious. Both errors tend to make him 'personal'" (SE, 10). The good poet should be conscious of the world as a world of moving particulars and unconscious of the creation of a new world. Blake, "a poet of genius" but not "a classic," was conscious of both the world of particulars and the creation of a new world of meaning. On the other hand, Swinburne, a much lesser poet, but still some kind of genius in Eliot's taxonomy, was unconscious of both, for he has no world whatever except for his world of words: in Swinburne's poetry "the object has ceased to exist, because the meaning is merely the hallucination of meaning. . . . Only a man of genius could dwell so exclusively and consistently among words as Swinburne" (SE, 285). Notice how object and meaning exist together for Eliot, who rejects Swinburne's world of words: "But the language which is more important to us is that which is struggling to digest and express new objects, new groups of objects, new feelings, new aspects, as, for instance, the prose of Mr. James Joyce or the earlier Conrad" (SE, 285).

III

If a poet is properly impersonal, properly aware of tradition, properly conscious and unconscious, then the poetry will have *form*. Understanding Eliot's peculiar definition of form is crucial for a practical and concrete understanding of the impersonal

theory of poetry. For Eliot, form is by no means the proper half of
the form/content dichotomy, nor is it an idealist notion of unity
and coherence, though these are aspects of a larger issue. Eliot himself struggled to clarify the meaning of form; his two most influential theoretical formulations outside of "Tradition and the Individual Talent"—that is, the "objective correlative" and the
"dissociation of sensibility"—arise from this struggle. *Form* and
formless are clearly two of Eliot's favorite critical terms, encompassing in the former impersonality, precision, presentation,
wholeness, and intellect, and in the latter personality, vagueness,
abstraction, fragmentation, and reflection. These terms do not respect the traditional form/content duality. Although Eliot sometimes distinguishes what is said from how it is said, he invariably
discusses both together or merely content alone; rarely does he discuss verbal mechanics apart from meaning. In *The Sacred Wood*
Eliot writes, "To create a form is not merely to invent a shape, a
rhyme or rhythm. It is also the realization of the whole appropriate
content of this rhyme or rhythm."[15] This realization of a whole and
appropriate content is a very precise idea for Eliot in the context of
his philosophy and critical theory. Throughout his early criticism,
Eliot provides negative and positive examples of this idea of form.

Eliot sees the defects in both Blake and Swinburne as defects of
form, even though their problems seem to be dramatically opposed.
But for both the weakness seems to be one of what is generally called
content. Eliot writes that "Swinburne's form is uninteresting, because he is literally saying next to nothing";[16] but for Blake, it is
taking his own philosophy too seriously which "makes him in-
clined to formlessness" (SE, 278). Eliot does not mean that Blake was
distracted by philosophy from the problems of language, for Blake
had "a remarkable and original sense of language and the music of
language" (SE, 279). But Blake was distracted from the problem of
form.

15. T. S. Eliot, "The Possibility of a Poetic Drama," *The Sacred Wood*, 63.
This book will hereinafter be cited parenthetically in the text as SW.
16. T. S. Eliot, "Isolated Superiority," *Dial*, LXXXIV (1928), 6. Quoted in Allan, *Impersonal Theory*, 137.

Eliot has more to say about philosophical poets. In his 1920 essay on Dante, Eliot argues against Valéry's rejection of philosophical poetry in favor of poetry which produces in us "a state." Eliot replies that the greatest poetry is a union of poetry and philosophy, as in Dante. However, poetry and philosophy are not the same thing:

> Without doubt, the effort of the philosopher proper, the man who is trying to deal with ideas in themselves, and the effort of the poet, who may be trying to *realize* ideas, cannot be carried on at the same time. But this is not to deny that poetry can be in some sense philosophic. The poet can deal with philosophic ideas, not as a matter for argument, but as matter for inspiration. The original form of philosophy cannot be poetic. (sw, 162)

This last sentence gives us a clue about Eliot's evaluation of Blake; Blake was concerned with developing an original philosophy and so was too much involved in ideas for their own sake, in argument, and in explanation. The poet should not develop ideas, but should *realize* (present) them. Poetry can only deal with a philosophic idea "when it has reached the point of immediate acceptance, when it has become almost a physical modification" (sw, 162–63). Eliot is not being anti-intellectual or eccentric in this. An idea can only be realized in a world which has been shaped by the idea. The idea must be embedded in the historical world, which is impersonal and temporal: "No man can invent a form, create a taste for it, and perfect it too" (sw, 62). No one has the time or the power to "create a taste" for a form (which is the realization of content), that is, to make an idea become so much a part of the world that it physically shapes the world and thus can be realized, not through one poet's imagination, but through the interpretive malleability of the world.

Eliot's argument against the merging of poetry and philosophy anticipates contemporary arguments about the activity of the critic/philosopher and the activity of the poet. The contemporary inclination is to remove distinctions between these activities because of the incessant metaphoricity of all language. Paul Ricoeur argues forcefully for the separation of speculative thought (distanciation) and poetry (appropriation), because each activity depends on the difference of the other. Without the differences, language moves toward a state of formless entropy.[17] Eliot's difficult argument against the confusion of philosophy and poetry also concerns form, and the distinction between his own critical and poetic writings is, perhaps, instructive.

This difference between philosophy and art can be clarified with more examples. In "The Possibility of a Poetic Drama" Eliot criticizes the demon in Goethe's *Faust* who, unlike Marlowe's Mephistopheles, embodies Goethe's own thoughts: "Goethe's demon inevitably sends us back to Goethe. He embodies a philosophy. A creation of art should not do that: he should *replace* the philosophy. . . . the drama is still a means" (sw, 66). Art that embodies an idea, rather than replacing it and making the ideal real, is too personal; it refers us to the author, to a "thinker." This art of "undigested" philosophy is also seen in "ordinary social comedy" such as that by Shaw or Galsworthy which "has some paltry idea or comment upon life put into the mouth of one of the characters at the end" (sw, 67). In this same essay, Eliot remarks that the undigested idea can also be found "in poetic dramas which are conscientious attempts to adopt a true structure, Athenian or Elizabethan, to contemporary feeling. It appears sometimes as the attempt to supply the defect of structure by an internal structure" (sw, 67). This odd statement reveals how far Eliot is from a conventional idea of structure (by which I believe he means, in this essay, form). If the structure of Elizabethan drama were only elements such as blank verse and five acts, then it could be adapted easily to modern drama. But these "external" elements only supply an "internal structure," not a true structure as they did in their own time. What is needed is "appropriate content," a "precise way of thinking and feeling" (sw, 63):

> The *framework* which was provided for the Elizabethan
> dramatist was not merely blank verse and the five-act play

---

17. Ricoeur, *Rule of Metaphor*, 257–313, is replying to Jacques Derrida, "White Mythology," trans. F. C. T. Moore, *New Literary History*, VI (1974), 5–74.

and the Elizabethan playhouse; it was not merely the plot
.... It was also the half-formed νλη, the "temper of the age"
(an unsatisfactory phrase), a preparedness, a habit on the
part of the public, to respond to particular stimuli. (sw, 63–
64)

Eliot is talking about convention here, but on a grand scale, since
for him "reality is a convention" (KE, 98). The acceptance of convention is not personal or even group choice; it is historical necessity. Form must be an absolute marriage of dramatic elements with
the *lived* thought of the time. Therefore, true structure, form, is external, in the world, not in a mental idea or imposed idea. In great
art the idea should "become so identified with the reality that you
can no longer say what the idea is" (sw, 68). The idea is transformed
into a world, into a "precise statement of life which is at the same
time a point of view, a world" (sw, 68).

This world presents itself in the poem as the affective quality of
being in this world, a quality of both emotion and thought. In
"Shakespeare and the Stoicism of Seneca," Eliot tells us that the
thought or philosophy which we think we find in great poets like
Dante or Shakespeare is really "the emotional equivalent of
thought," and the great artists differ from the lesser not because of
"a difference in the quality of thought, but a difference in the quality of emotion" (SE, 115). The emphasis on emotion is partly a cor-
rective to the defect of undigested philosophy, but we are not to
identify form with our usual notion of emotion. For the undigested
ideas are only one cause of formlessness. The opposite defect, and
possibly the more common object of Eliot's criticism, is the defect
of imprecise and inexpressible emotion: "We talk as if thought was
precise and emotion was vague. In reality there is precise emotion
and there is vague emotion. To express precise emotion requires as
great intellectual power as to express precise thought" (SE, 115).
Vague emotions are personal emotions or psychic states which in
themselves are illusory, cut off from reality, and inappropriate for
art (though not meaningless in our life, since in our errancy we naturally deal with the self as a real thing). Precise thought, too, is only
a fragment of reality, at its best explaining but not presenting real-

ity, and inappropriate for art. Precise emotion, on the other hand, is a being-in-the-world, a concrete point of view which is neither subjective and personal, nor objective and empirical. Precise emotion is shaped by and shaping of a world which is itself realized ideas. Precise emotion is the contact of a particular historical moment with tradition, so that it is unique but never idiosyncratic, human but never subjective, meaningful but never an idea. The hermeneutic relationship between the particular point of view (non-subjective) and the tradition always exists as world, but is presented only in great art.

In his essay on Shakespeare Eliot expresses this hermeneutic complexity. Art presents not *a* meaning but the meaningfulness of a world shaped by human concerns: "I would suggest that none of the plays of Shakespeare has a 'meaning,' although it would be equally false to say that a play of Shakespeare is meaningless" (SE, 115). The meaningfulness is "emotional" and "cannot be defined adequately in intellectual terms" (SE, 118), because it cannot be compartmentalized. A poet should "express the greatest emotional intensity of his time," but also "some permanent human impulse," and himself: "The great poet, in writing himself, writes his time" (SE, 117). These are basically the same three elements of "Tradition and the Individual Talent." The permanent, the historical, and the individual form a hermeneutic circle, each determining and determined by the other. Separating out just the permanent idea or the personal emotion destroys art. The whole circle is presented in "precise emotion."

Eliot finds that much art, even good (though never great) art provides vague emotion rather than precise emotion, a perception that leads him to formulate the ideas of the "objective correlative" and "dissociation of sensibility." In the famous essay on *Hamlet* (1919), Eliot observes that the problem of both Hamlet and Shakespeare is one of "bafflement" at their inability to find an objective equivalent to their feelings: "Hamlet (the man) is dominated by an emotion which is inexpressible, because it is in *excess* of the facts as they appear" (SE, 125). Well, what is wrong with this? Eliot answers this question most clearly in a later essay where he again objects to an artist's bafflement.[18] In "Lancelot Andrewes" (1926) Eliot finds Donne's sermons to be "baffling," "vague and unformed": "He is a little of the religious spellbinder, the Reverend Billy Sunday of his time, the flesh-creeper, the sorcerer of emotional orgy" (SE, 302). Donne's problem as a preacher is that he "is a 'personality' . . . his sermons, one feels, are a 'means of self-expression.' He is constantly finding an object which shall be adequate to his feelings" (SE, 309). On the other hand, "Andrewes is wholly absorbed in the object and therefore responds with the adequate emotion" (SE, 309); "Andrewes's emotion is purely contemplative; it is not personal, it is wholly evoked by the object of contemplation, to which it is adequate; his emotions wholly contained in and explained by its object" (SE, 308–309). To Eliot, Donne has an inner state which he is trying to express; but since no object seems entirely to mirror an inner state, he must use language that is vague, too personal, extraneously emotional. The defect is in taking an inner state as the primary reality, rather than the world. Donne is "primarily interested in man" and in this he is, compared to Andrewes, "the more modern" (SE, 309). He is, however, the lesser theologian in Eliot's mind.

When emotion precedes or exceeds the object in art, we do not have a world being presented, but only a fragment of a whole, a secondary creation called personality. Just as earlier we saw that meaning cannot exceed existence for Eliot, so emotion should not exceed the object. Their interdependence must be total:

> The only way of expressing emotion in the form of art is by finding an "objective correlative"; in other words, a set of objects, a situation, a chain of events which shall be the formula of that *particular* emotion; such that when the external facts, which must terminate in sensory experience, are given, the emotion is immediately evoked. (SE, 124–25)

Eliot is not as clear in this famous statement as in his criticism of Donne about the nontemporal precedence of object over emotion:

18. Again, in "Francis Herbert Bradley" Eliot writes, "One feels that the emotional intensity of Ruskin is partly a deflection of something that was baffled in life (SE, 395).

the emotion must be wholly adequate and inevitable for the object, not the object for the emotion. Our romantic prejudice suggests to us that the artist has a feeling and then looks around for a way to express it. But for Eliot the emotion is not in us, but in the world, inhering in the object as that object is for us. That is, the objective correlative is in no way an empirical object which through its rigidity will give form to emotions. The form is that union of object and emotion in a world. Because Hamlet's emotion, according to Eliot, seems out of proportion to the events of the play, we are led to speculate about his inner state, and the play becomes a psychological problem, not art. Our attention is focused too much on the some*thing* that is not being expressed, not on the infinitely more complicated hermeneutic process revealed in precise emotion.

In spite of the examples of Donne and Shakespeare, Eliot finds this defect of vague emotion mostly in romantic writers from the eighteenth century on, leading him to speculate that there has been a change in human thinking from classical to modern times. He pinpoints this change in the seventeenth century and calls it a "dissociation of sensibility." The metaphysical poets, like the artists before them, had a sensibility "which could devour any kind of experience"; they could "feel their thought as immediately as the odour of a rose" (SE, 247). For Donne, whose poetry does not to Eliot share the defects of his sermons, "a thought . . . was an experience; it modified his sensibility" (SE, 247). After the seventeenth century, emotions become cut off from thought and the world and are reified into the modern "personality" or "self," a permanent emotional disposition not modified by anything. Eliot's observation is not new to us today.[19] The rationalism and the empiricism beginning in the seventeenth century separated the subjective from the

19. Michel Foucault, in *The Order of Things: An Archeology of the Human Sciences* (New York, 1973), has a brilliant analysis of the changes in human sensibility, or episteme, as he calls it. He, too, finds a change of sensibility in the seventeenth century, as well as one in the nineteenth century, both of which contribute to the separation of subject from object and to the reification of the idea of self. This summary considerably simplifies the complex work of Foucault, but I only wish to suggest how Eliot's idea foreshadows some of our most interesting contemporary philosophy.

objective, concentrating on the objective, and the romantics' reassertion of feeling was only a further acceptance of this fragmented situation of inner states unconnected to external objects. However different the eighteenth and nineteenth centuries might have been, they both for Eliot are responsible for creating the self and for directing interest primarily to man. The result, for art, of dissociating sensibility is that "the feeling became more crude. The feeling, the sensibility, expressed in the *Country Churchyard* (to say nothing of Tennyson and Browning) is cruder than that in the *Coy Mistress*" (SE, 247). Relegating feeling within the rigid boundary of a personality is bound to constrain it; it will then have the enriching complexity of neither the present world nor the tradition. Thought in dissociated poetry is only appropriate as something to reflect upon with a sensitive personality. Rather than realizing ideas in poetry, these poets "merely meditate on them poetically" (SE, 248). The creation of self was the beginning of sentimentality:

> The sentimental age began early in the eighteenth century, and continued. The poets revolted against the ratiocinative, the descriptive; they thought and felt by fits, unbalanced; they reflected. In one or two passages of Shelley's *Triumph of Life*, in the second *Hyperion*, there are traces of a struggle toward unification of sensibility. But Keats and Shelley died, and Tennyson and Browning ruminated. (SE, 248)

The poetry of these artists is overly personal and formless, for "the nineteenth century had a good many fresh impressions; but it had no forms in which to confine them" (SW, 62). For Eliot form as the impersonal, as the precise emotion, is sadly lacking in most romantic efforts.

Eliot sees that most modern poetry remains that of a dissociated sensibility. As Eliot tells us in "Dante" (1920), Valéry, trying to escape the rumination of the Victorians, declares that poetry should "produce in us a state." Eliot's reply is apropos to much of the foregoing discussion:

> A state, in itself is nothing whatever. . . . The poet does not aim to excite—that is not even a test of his success—but to set something down; the state of the reader is merely that reader's particular mode of perceiving what the poet has caught in words. Dante, more than any other poet, has succeeded in dealing with his philosophy, not as a theory . . . or as his own comment or reflection, but in terms of something *perceived*. When most of our modern poets confine themselves to what they had perceived, they produce for us, usually, only odds and ends of still life and stage properties; but that does not imply so much that the method of Dante is obsolete, as that our vision is perhaps comparatively restricted. (sw, 170–71).

Neither an idea, nor an emotional state, nor an emotional reflection on an idea, poetry is a presentation of a world which is non-subjective, real, historical, traditional, an "objective" realization of idea and emotion. With form, with precise emotion, the world of the poem is whole and self-contained because it doesn't refer to anything else, as *Hamlet* refers to an un*real*ized emotion and some of Blake refers to an un*real*ized philosophy. But this world is meaningful, as immediately and untranslatably meaningful as "the odour of a rose." The world of the poem is also a particular point of view on the world, a "finite centre," a particular interpretation. The Absolute is nowhere to be found. Even Eliot's beloved *Paradiso* presents blessedness "sensuously" (se, 226); Dante could "realize the inapprehensible in visual images" (se, 228). The poem is flexible, rich with possibility, which arises only from presenting existence, not essence. The metaphoric activity of Dante's poem, which presents the real, depends upon the lack of essences, the absence of presence guaranteed by human finitude. The word has the autonomy to change with time so that the real, that mystery of existence lost in the clarity of essence, can be presented in language.

Chapter Five

The Waste Land: A Ceaseless Hermeneutic

And the world, as we have seen, exists only as it is found in the experiences of finite centres, experiences so mad and strange that they will be boiled away before you boil them down to one homogeneous mass.

T. S. Eliot
Knowledge and Experience

I

In 1922 even the devoted reader of Eliot's first two volumes of poetry could not have been prepared for a poem like *The Waste Land*. Eliot's earlier poems are divided between the impressionistic eye and the satiric eye, but always a narrative persona interests us. Only in "Gerontion" is there a clash of voices which struggle to escape the confines of a stated subjectivity, trapped between "Here I am, an old man in a dry month" and "Thoughts of a dry brain in a dry season."[1] Eliot wanted to include "Gerontion" in *The Waste Land* (but was dissuaded by Pound), perhaps as much to

1. T. S. Eliot, *Collected Poems 1909–1962* (New York, 1963), 29, 31. Hereinafter cited parenthetically in the text as CP. All lines of poetry quoted in this chapter and referenced only by line numbers are from *The Waste Land*, CP, 51–76.

question the neat boundaries of "Gerontion" as to complement the material of *The Waste Land.*

The sensibility in these early poems is always a unique one, observing the world from a very particular point of view, which is never sentimental, abstract, or ruminating. The poet is interested in the world's complexity, so oppressive to Prufrock and so invisible to Sweeney. But the poet masters the world with the work, rendering the subtle nuances of human life with carefully controlled rhythms and images, and ridiculing the simpleminded and the pretentious with the deflating power of satiric diction. The poems strike the reader from their first lines with their particular and pointed observations: "The winter evening settles down / With smell of steaks in passageways. / Six o'clock" ("Preludes," CP, 13) or "Apeneck Sweeney spreads his knees / Letting his arms hang down to laugh" ("Sweeney Among the Nightingales," CP, 49). The subject is in control of his object; the individual talent is displayed.

How different and disconcerting to read:

> April is the cruelest month, breeding
> Lilacs out of the dead land, mixing
> Memory and desire, stirring
> Dull roots with spring rain.
> Winter kept us warm, covering
> Earth in forgetful snow, feeding
> A little life with dried tubers. (ll. 1–7)

These lines are at once more general and less accessible than the openings of Eliot's earlier poems. This is not the unique sensibility playing on an object, for neither sensibility nor object seem defined. The invocation to spring is broadly universal and cultural: "Whan that Aprill with his shoures soote. . . . " Even the inversion of sentiment is no surprise to the reader of Whitman:

> When lilacs last in the dooryard bloom'd,
> And the great star early droop'd in the western sky in the
>   night,
> I mourn'd and yet shall mourn with ever-returning spring.

The theme of Eliot's lines is fertility, the diction is plain, the re-petitive rhythm is incantatory—the halting verbals ending each line echo like a ritual chorus. This is not the language of personal impressionism or satire, but is perhaps best described by a later poem of Eliot's as "the abstract conception / Of private experience at its greatest intensity / Becoming universal" ("A Note on War Poetry," CP, 216).

Yet the harshness and malaise in the opening lines of *The Waste Land* are distinctly of a particular historical time of existential anxiety. The tradition takes up, is taken up by, the century defined by a devastating world war and a loss of faith in God and rationality, giving us angst about April, about growth, about time (that union of memory and desire in our present). But these declamatory lines will not provide any stability against this angst. Suddenly the syntax shifts *gestalts*, mutating into the incidental and chatty: "Summer surprised us, coming over the Starnbergersee / With a shower of rain ..." (ll. 8–9). This narrative about Munich hardly seems connected to the opening seven lines. The portentous generality with which spring and winter are interpreted gives way to a particular and neutral interpretation of summer, breaking out of the control of the rhetoric, the logic, and the idea. There is no center here, only generation, which is the initial source of the anxiety. The shift of voice accomplished by a syntactical metonymy is both disturbing and liberating, confirming anxiety in the mechanism of displacement, but also diffusing it in the errancy of the particular.

By the end of the poem, the spring rain will undergo an interpretive metamorphosis from a cruel to a saving release, as generation and interpretation are chosen over sterility and rigidity. Then, the meaningless repetition of the spring thunder is interpreted in three ways and these three commands form an invitation to the give and take of hermeneutic experience—give, sympathize, control; and each command is further diffused into the opaque particularity of lyric interpretations. The anxiety caused by the lack of clarity throughout the poem is hermeneutically attached to the freedom from rigidity which this density affords. Could we find a situation that more wholly contains this union of fear and freedom than:

> And when we were children, staying at the arch-duke's,
> My cousin's, he took me out on a sled,
> And I was frightened. He said, Marie,
> Marie, hold on tight. And down we went.
> In the mountains, there you feel free. (11. 13–17)

This is "precise emotion."

The Waste Land is the fruit of Eliot's early critical work. It is both more conscious of tradition than his first volume of poetry—*Prufrock and Other Observations* (1917)—and less conscious of the self than the satires of the second volume—*Poems* (1919). By presenting an historical cultural world, not a subjective world, *The Waste Land* presents neither undigested philosophy nor vague emotion. The lyric voice of the poem is only one among many narrative, dramatic, and prophetic voices. Here, the artifacts of modernity—the motorcars, gramophones,typists, crowds, nerves—exist alongside the artifacts of culture—Shakespeare, Dante, Spenser, the Bible. No one thing seems privileged in this world as a central meaning. In particular, the voices of culture do not provide any overall framework, since they, too, are woven into the texture of the world, not kept apart as a comment on this world. The culture is not in the past; as Eliot taught us, only because tradition is present is it part of our world. For no one in Spenser's day did the Thames contain the meaning, "Sweet Thames, run softly, till I end my song" (l. 177). Only since Spenser's "Prothalamion" is the world so enriched. The poem makes nostalgia impossible because of the blending of present and past. The world of the poem would not exist without the cultural allusions; and the meaning of the allusions is as completely dependent on the present as the present is on its cultural heritage. The poet is, indeed, wholly absorbed into his object, so that it is the cultural world which speaks and which provides the ideas and emotions, not a persona. The poem has *form* in Eliot's sense.

The density and complexity of the poem and the corresponding absence of finality are in some sense untranslatable into rational discourse because rational enclosure is precisely what the poem avoids. Still, I would like to suggest some avenues for interpretation of this difficult poem based on the hermeneutic ideas of the earlier chapters. My reading is by no means a complete explication of the poem. Rather, I have chosen a few examples from the poem to display the larger principles of a hermeneutic view of world and self. First, I will give a brief overview of the poem as a presentation of hermeneutic existence. Then, I will examine some poetic techniques which do the work of presentation, specifically metonymy, narrative, and allusion. Then, in what may seem at first like a digression, I would like to explain the hermeneutic analysis of the psyche based on the theories of Jacques Lacan in order to account for the poem's persistent interest in relationships, particularly sexual relationships. The relationships between self and other and between love and death are crucial for the poem as a whole. Finally, I hope to gather up these interpretive strands in an analysis of the final section of the poem, "What the Thunder Said."

I do not plan to discuss the manuscript version of *The Waste Land*, which was published in 1971,[2] because I am more interested in the poem which has interacted with our culture, that is, the original 1922 version. For all of the arguments I have advanced about Eliot's aesthetic theory, I am not making an argument about Eliot's intentions, but about an historical *Zeitgeist*. The poem as first published said something to its own time and continues to be a presence in our time. That Pound could understand the force of Eliot's poem is only evidence for its cultural meaning. I do not, however, believe that Pound was responsible for the innovations in *The Waste Land*. An examination of the manuscript shows that, apart from a few minor revisions in diction, Pound's contributions were the removal of two long sections beginning "The Fire Sermon" and "Death by Water" and rather extensive revisions of the teatime episode in "The Fire Sermon." The long section at the beginning of the poem seems to have been excised by Eliot himself.

Pound certainly did the world a favor by removing the satiric

---

2. T. S. Eliot, *"The Waste Land": A Facsimile and Transcript of the Original Drafts Including the Annotations of Ezra Pound*, ed. Valerie Eliot (New York, 1971).

Fresca episode and reworking the original teatime episode, both of which, like many of Eliot's satires, are grating and tasteless. Eliot seems to have abandoned this sort of satire in poetry after *The Waste Land*, whether under the influence of Pound or religion, and we can only be grateful. But the strategy of the poem and the most powerful passages in the poem are not disturbed by Pound. The cut passages give us more voices and more narrative, but no more logical connections than in the published version. Section V is untouched by Pound (according to the manuscript edition), as are the remaining stanzas of Section IV and the beginning and end of Section III. And many of Pound's minor suggestions in Sections I and II are rejected by Eliot. *The Waste Land* is, in my opinion, a better poem for Pound's advice (and, we must remember, for Eliot's understanding that the poem was not inviolably his own), but the draft version is not different in its entelechy from the published version.

By avoiding the onus of either idea or personality, *The Waste Land* is at once highly intellectual and purely emotional, because "precise emotion" is totally realized in the objects of the poem. That is, the world of the poem wholly contains any idea or emotion which could be inferred from the poem. We could even say that the density of the poem exceeds the limitation of idea or sensibility. Yet the poem is clearly informed by idea, even though one would be hard pressed to find a line of undigested philosophy in the poem, and by emotion, even though the emotion does not emanate from a personality. The poem presents a world defined by the absence of a central stabilizing force, whether God, logic, the self, or empirical certainty. Without this center, the world has no order or delimitation among objects, subjects, ideas, emotions, past, or present. The situation is one of being-in-the-world. In the absence of essence, self and world define each other diacritically; the self is made up of social, cultural, existential forces, while the world exists *for* us (even in its horrors) as the meaningful arrangement of human interpretations. Being-in-the-world is the ongoing process of interpretation in the face of change and finitude.

The Waste Land begins with the paradox most basic to human existence, the absolute interdependence of life and death. The first lines present the inevitability of generation in the movement of the seasons, where the projection of our desire to be sufficient gathers up the memory of our thrown, insufficient, finite state into the hermeneutic of time. But the poem tries to reject this hermeneutic foundation by separating desire from memory. The poem is full of anxiety about death and generation, and aching with desire for a separation from our limitation and finitude. But every separation from memory and a world (even a bad world) is sterile and barren, a fate worse than death. Like the Sibyl in her prison of immortality, with lack of death there remains no desire except for death: " . . . she would always respond: 'I yearn to die.'"[3] Throughout the poem, the worst horror is reserved for the barren, changeless environments devoid of a human life of pain and death. The human world is, in contrast, full of meaningful fragments, a vast sea in which no one survives.

This simple duality in the poem is not so simple, for the hermeneutic world resists and defeats this duality. The human world is created in the desire to escape the absence defining our existence. The symbols, myths, art, and all of society attempt, in the endless elaboration of a relational linguistic world, to cover the absence. Lacan identifies this human activity as the "metonymy of desire,"[4] which reveals our lack of wholeness and sufficiency even while it tries to hide this lack. Human life is a constant conjunction of death and desire to escape death. We are never purely toward death, without the errancy of our desire. *Errancy* is a key term from Heidegger which will serve to focus several issues here. Errancy is the inevitable human condition of being able to know only particular beings and never Being as a whole. Our desire to know Being as a whole— something changeless, eternal, and complete—and thus escape from change, finitude, and absence can only be manifest in beings which are themselves finite. In *The Waste Land* the attempt to achieve

3. Epigraph to *The Waste Land* from Petronius, *Satyricon*, chapter 48, translated by George Williamson, *A Reader's Guide to T. S. Eliot*, 129.
4. This phrase actually comes from the famous article on Lacan by Jean Laplanche and Serge Leclaire, "L'Inconscient," *Les Temps Modernes*, XVII (July, 1961), 81–129.

some metaphoric/symbolic enclosure (or presence) is undercut by metonymic particularity, allusive dispersion, and constant meta- morphosis. While the poem desires presence, the desire produces only particularity and absence. We cannot escape our errancy; we can only recognize and accept the always fragmentary and herme- neutic nature of human being. The search for presence, which if achieved would bring only sterility and imprisonment in a fixed and isolated self, is possible only because of the freedom residing in the absence which allows beings to be. The poem, especially the end of the poem, presents a world imbued with our desire for changeless- ness, even while it shows our finitude. We cannot just reject the sterility of a quest for changelessness and embrace our finitude. The acceptance must be of a world of desire and death where questing is a way of life which continually discovers only the necessity for the quest.

II

This brief overview of issues in *The Waste Land* will serve to frame a more specific discussion of techniques of the poem that present the absence of essence underlying death and desire. Formally, the poem conspicuously lacks the features of language which limit and define meaning. The various episodes and passages in the poem appear to have no logical connection, syntax is often disjointed, constant allusion defers and diffuses meaning. If this overriding parataxis were not enough to dispel the illusion of a center, especially a controlling consciousness, the poem also speaks in various dramatic voices, and, in passages of description, predic- ation is often given to the object rather than to an observing nar- rator.

Those voices with a specified and limited identity include the Lithuanian, Marie, the hyacinth girl, Madame Sosostris, the ner- vous woman, the woman in the pub, Tiresias, the three Thames- daughters, and—in the nonhuman category—the nightingale, "Twit twit twit / Jug jug jug jug jug jug," the hermit thrush, "Drip drop drip drop drop drop drop," the cock, "Coco rico co co rico," and the thunder, "Da." These voices are clearly different from the prophetic voice of the opening lines, the red rock section, and the opening to section V, which speaks in repetitive, nonprogressive syntax and symbolic, nonspecific images. These voices are also distinguished from the general narrative voice, whose identity is often obscured by the allusions and by the poem's tendency to ascribe the action to the object, not to an observing I.

For instance, in the opening to "A Game of Chess" the long passage of description both affirms the sense of being in a human world and denies the sense of a personality. The structure of the description follows the movement of an eye from the marble floor to the coffered ceiling to the fireplace, attracted by the point of light. We are *placed* in an environment by this movement. But all of the movement and life is ascribed to the objects of the room: the glass "Doubled the flames of seven branched candelabra / Reflecting light upon the table as / The glitter of jewels rose to meet it, / From satin cases poured in rich profusion" (ll. 82–85). Their perfumes "lurked," odors "ascended," flames "flung their smoke into the laquearia, / Stirring the pattern on the coffered ceiling" (ll. 92–93). The whole scene is synaesthetically animated through the objects themselves, which do not seem to be dependent on an experiencing subject for their life. The allusions in this passage to *Antony and Cleopatra* and the *Aeneid* further distance the passage from a unique sensibility by placing the objects in a cultural and not a personal system of meaning.

This same technique is used in the teatime episode in "The Fire Sermon." There, the syntax robs the typist of her subjectivity by ascribing human actions to the environment:

> At the violet hour, the evening hour that strives
> Homeward, and brings the sailor home from the sea,
> The typist home at teatime, clears her breakfast, lights
> Her stove, and lays out food in tins.
> Out of the window perilously spread
> Her drying combinations touched by the sun's last rays,

> On the divan are piled (at night her bed)
> Stockings, slippers, camisoles, and stays. (ll. 220–27)

In the first part of this passage, all of the verbs—*strives, brings, clears, lights, lays*—are syntactically bound to the subject "evening hour" rather than to the expected subject, the typist. In the last four lines, the passive constructions focus upon the typist's clothes, not on the person. Again, the environment is animated, the source of a particular life, while the typist herself is without intentionality. When the woman is allowed to be a subject, she does not have as much personality as her environment; she is universalized in an allusion to Goldsmith:

> When lovely woman stoops to folly and
> Paces about her room again, alone,
> She smoothes her hair with automatic hand,
> And puts a record on the gramophone. (ll. 253–56)

The woman's actions are mechanized by the juxtaposition of her "automatic hand" with the mechanical arm of the gramophone, just as earlier in this episode the human and mechanical are merged: ". . . the human engine waits / Like a taxi throbbing waiting" (ll. 216–17). This entire scene, which so drains the woman of an autonomous self, is given to us in the voice of Tiresias, that blind prophet, part man, part woman. Eliot's curious note about Tiresias has inspired many "suspicious" interpretations of this poem: "What Tiresias *sees*, in fact, is the substance of the poem" (cp, 72). Being blind, Tiresias actually sees nothing, but in escaping the limitations of finitude, Tiresias can see the absence which human errancy obscures. More specifically, the teatime episode does reveal in part the substance of the poem. The sordid and indifferent sex scene presents the sad shortcomings of human desire, which is, I will argue, Eliot's central image for man's state as a creature of finite limitation and infinite desire. In addition, what Tiresias sees is how things are "throbbing," motivated by the absence of essence and the power of desire. In merging the typist with her landscape, Tiresias reveals how little there is a self apart from the world and how little control the human has over the throbbing nature of reality.

This recognition by Tiresias reveals how different he is from some of the less distanced narrators of the poem. The frequent use of "I" by both dramatized characters and unspecified narrative voices reminds us of the impossibility of escaping finite particularity—Eliot's finite center or point of view—which is not, however, a coherent or controlling self. The opacity of these voices, whether due to their allusiveness, or their empirical triviality, or their lack of semantic content ("Ta ta" as well as "Jug jug"), or their human foreignness (for those who do not know German, French, Italian, and Sanskrit), continues to undermine the idea of self as "presence" and to allow metamorphosis from one "I" to the next.[5]

A further complication in our search for a persona is the inclusion of the notes in the first book edition of the poem. Not finding a coherent center of meaning in the poem, readers are referred out of the poem to "explanatory" notes, which suggest that the center of meaning is in Eliot himself. But the notes also defer meaning into more fragmentation. Most of the notes refer the reader to yet another text or offer an extended quotation from the original, often untranslated, text (another voice). These notes may give the reader at best a partial knowledge of what allusions exist in the poem, but they offer few clues to the coherence of these allusions.

Some readers have found these notes positively misleading because of their selectivity and, often, eccentricity.[6] For instance, the reference to the delusions of the Antarctic explorers seems irrelevant and excessive since we have already been given the seemingly more appropriate reference to Christ on the road to Emmaus. But the note to "with a dead sound on the final stroke of nine" (l. 68) tells us only that the sound is "a phenomenon I have often noted," ignoring the richer allusion to the crucifixion occurring at the ninth hour. The careful explication of "C.i.f." and the prosaic reference

5. See Charles Tomlinson, *Poetry and Metamorphosis* (New York, 1983), 23–47.
6. Ruth Nevo, "*The Waste Land*: Ur Text of Deconstruction," *New Literary History*, XIII (1982), 459.

to *The Proposed Demolition of Nineteen City Churches* in the note to the mysterious and beautiful lines about St. Magnus Martyr seem to be playing a totally different and more empirical language game than most of the other notes. The long quotation from Bradley has caused more trouble than clarity, while the note about the hermit thrush introduces both obscurity ("This is *Turdus aonalaschkae pallasii*") and over-simplification, "Its 'water-dripping song' is justly celebrated" (CP, 74). In these two notes, Eliot allows a philosopher and an ornithologist to speak for him, only extending the range of voices we hear in the poem. Far from supplying evidence of a controlling "I", these notes only give us evidence of the limitations of a human consciousness. Eliot the note writer and explainer is woefully inadequate to the poem and is clearly different from the poem.

Faced with the fragmentation of both the coherent world, in the lack of logic and causation, and the coherent persona, in the many voices, the reader assumes that the poem's meaning must be symbolic, based on a metaphoric relationship between episodes. But the juxtapositions in the poem rarely seem to resolve into a unity; the implied comparisons are at best a violent catachresis. In *The Waste Land* the density of the literal meaning impels us toward a clear figurative meaning or idea for explanation. In this hermeneutics of suspicion the whole poem becomes a metaphor for spiritual death and rebirth or some such theme. But the poem seems to reject the metaphysics of essence implied by this metaphoric interpretation. *The Waste Land* bears little similarity to the symbolist poem which often uses elaborate metaphors to present a world of spirit or mind totally removed from the world we live in. Eliot's poem uses only a few metaphors at all (except the implied comparison of personification) and is rather deeply concerned with the existing world of 1920. Mainly, its parataxis creates the need for metaphoric unity, but Eliot's own rejection of essence in his prose writings suggests that the existence of the details is not to be submerged in a unity of idea.

For instance, in "The Burial of the Dead," a section with many juxtapositions of different material, the various episodes are often considered by critics to be symbolically united under the ideas of death and fear; only the Munich episode (ll. 8–12) seems to have no relation to death. But this symbolic explanation explains very little about this dense section of *The Waste Land*. In fact, the symbolic reading seems appropriate only for the opening invocation, the red rock episode, parts of the Tristan and Isolde section, and the Unreal City episode. In these sections, the repetitive syntax and surreal images cry out for symbolic interpretation. But the narrative and dramatic particularity of the other episodes (the Munich episode, the Marie episode, the Tristan and Isolde episode, the Madame Sosostris episode, and the Stetson episode) escapes a metaphoric reading. Throughout the rest of the poem, only the long opening to section V and several episodes in section III also seem heavily symbolic. At most, these sections make up only half of the poem. Taken alone, the symbolic images of the barren waste and the incantatory repetition of syntax form a powerful symbolic evocation of a rejection of the human world. In these symbolic passages there is an absence of culture, of meaningful movement, of life. These images have been most important in the critical readings of the poem. But the symbolic "Nothing again nothing" (l. 120) is matched or exceeded in power by the more subliminal effects of the narrative sections. These narratives offer a vital alternative, which does not cancel the nothingness but uses it, finding life in absence.

I would argue that equally as important as the symbolic evocation of changelessness is the metonymic narrative presentation of the opaqueness of the human world. Following Roman Jakobson, current fashion divides the functioning of language into the metaphoric pole of substitution and similarity, mainly involving objects, and the metonymic pole of combination and contiguity, mainly involving relations.[7] Jakobson categorized forms of art according to this model so that romanticism and symbolism (and surrealism) are metaphoric, and realism and cubism are metonymic. While I will insist that a rigid duality is artificial and that meta-

7. Ricoeur, *The Rule of Metaphor*, 174–80, discusses Jakobson's article "Two Aspects of Language and Two Types of Aphasic Disturbances," originally in R. Jakobson and M. Halle, *The Fundamentals of Language* (The Hague, 1956).

phoric and metonymic functions always interact hermeneutically, in *The Waste Land* this structural division provides a helpful criticism of the unbalanced metaphoric readings of the poem.

III

It hardly seems necessary to say that relations which cannot be explained by similarity may be explained by contiguity. Jakobson believed that because metaphor is easier to grasp conceptually than metonymy, the function of metonymy has long been ignored. Metonymy is preeminently the figure of narrative, establishing relationships of contiguity between events, characters, setting, and atmosphere. Metonymy places things in meaningful relation and thus in a world; metonymy also presents time. The large amount of narrative in *The Waste Land* has usually been subordinated in criticism to the metaphoric symbolism, but perhaps the metaphoric should be subordinated to the metonymic world and time. For it is the narrative voices which are so unusual in this poem; they keep the poem grounded in a world and not floating away from the here and now of human concerns into symbolic or linguistic solipsism. We may even draw a parallel between the hermeneutic relationship in language between autonomy and ontological grounding and the relationship between metaphoric and metonymic techniques in *The Waste Land*. The metaphoric function undercuts the illusion of reference to a fixed object or consciousness, while metonymy gives the poem a relational world.

The narrative in *The Waste Land*, especially the narrative dialogue, is strikingly natural given the exigency of meter; Eliot's talent for realistic dialogue in meter is well exhibited in the verse drama. To understand the meaningful movement of the narrative in this poem, one has only to compare a narrative section with a symbolic section. Looking again at the opening lines of "The Burial of the Dead," we find that the first seven lines differ from the succeeding nine lines in both world and time. That is, in the first passage each detail is carefully chosen for symbolic force: "lilacs," "dull roots," "spring rain," "dried tubers"—this constellation of images has symbolic force even without the rest of the poem to reinforce it. But in the narrative episode the details have no such force in their own section or in the rest of the poem: "colonnade," "Hofgarten," "coffee," "sled," even, I would argue, the line in German—these are the metonymic details which make up a narrative world that is dense, particular, and inexplicable.

Similarly, the movement through time in the first passage is stymied by the separation of the participles from their objects, emphasizing the timeless quality of "breeding," "mixing," "stirring," "covering," and "feeding." These lines speak of a general and permanent state. This generality is even more emphasized by the contrasting use of the same syntax for specific narrative purposes: "Summer surprised us, coming over the Starnbergersee / With a shower of rain." The participle is now connected to its object and placed in a specific time of events. We may read the lines as meaning that *we* were coming over the Starnbergersee or the *rain* was coming over the Starnbergersee; in either case, the duration of action is limited, for "we stopped in the colonnade, / And went on in sunlight, into the Hofgarten, / And drank coffee, and talked for an hour" (ll. 9–11). The series of consecutive events gives the feeling of meaningful time, the time in which to do something, as opposed to the time of empty repetition as in the opening seven lines of the poem.

According to Ricoeur's analysis of narrative in terms of Heideggerian time, narrative presents significant world-time, not the abstract series of nows which is generally taken to be time.[8] This time in which to do something is ontologically based most clearly in the movement of the sun, in the days which, for us, are numbered, and yet in which we have time *for* something. Eliot images the purposeful anxiety of world-time in the lines: "Your shadow at morning striding behind you / Or your shadow at evening rising to meet you" (ll. 28–29). This time is compared to the static time of the

8. Paul Ricoeur, "Narrative Time," *Critical Inquiry*, VII (Autumn, 1980), 169–90.

symbolic shadow under the symbolic rock where life has returned to "a handful of dust" (l. 30).

Narrative places the reader in the Heideggerian skein of future, past, present which together constitute time. A narrative is directed toward the future, the direction of concern; the end of the narrative draws the reader toward it. But a sense of thrownness (the past) always inheres in this forward movement. That is, the move toward an end, which would uncover the pattern inherent in the events, is impeded by the contingency of the given world which retains its interpretive richness in spite of the pattern which is finally imposed upon it by an ending. Ricoeur insists that this second dimension of narrative is never dispelled by the first. Even in a known narrative, like a folk tale, the knowledge of the end cannot make the narrative a static configuration. Many structuralists reify the structural interpretation of events, dismissing time as an abstract progression not integral to the structure of events. Ricoeur points out that this structural analysis creates a "logical matrix" of the narrative, "a machinery whose task it is to compensate for the initial mischief or lack by a final restoration of disturbed order."[9] The model Ricoeur attacks is based upon the quest myth as central to all narrative; for the structuralists, the perfect order exists prior to the change or lack which makes the quest necessary, and this order is restored at the end of the quest. But in a temporal analysis of quest narrative, the lack precedes and causes the final "order." This order does not abolish the lack, because the order is only constituted of the possibilities which were in the events all along. Any order we see in a narrative is a result of the projection toward an ending combined with the contingency of the details. The order arises because of the lack which begins the quest and must necessarily contain that lack. All narratives are based on the quest myth because of the absence of order inherent in the quest which forms the opacity of the narrative. Narrative is, in turn, central to the quest myth, because only narrative presents the opacity of the world which is time and finitude.[10]

9. *Ibid.*, 184.
10. See Paul Ricoeur, *The Symbolism of Evil*, trans. Emerson Buchanan (Boston, 1969), 162–3, for a discussion of myth and narrative.

The quest myth is the ur-tale of interpretive being. The fertile land is created from the waste by the quest, but, as is evident from Jessie Weston's book, the quester in the myth generally does not know the object of the quest, certainly does not know how to reach the goal, and is usually unaware of what he has done to bring fertility to the land. Often asking questions is enough to fight the barrenness—no answers are necessary, because none are available. The goal of the quest seems to be the quest itself. The confusing and inexplicable journey of the quester is the activity of being-in-the-world—the body becomes the land. In the quest, the desire for presence is never fulfilled, but the land is restored nevertheless. The restorative magic remains an absence.

The use of the quest myth in *The Waste Land* points up the enigmatic quality of the quest. As Eliot emphasizes in his notes, the quest imagery provides a symbolic matrix for the poem with the wasted land, the fisher king, the chapel perilous, and the ritual death by water. But in the poem, the symbols do not cohere. Not only is fertility not desired at the beginning of the poem, but the possibility of a mythical order in the poem is undercut by the constant intervention of the social and cultural world, particularly in the first three sections of the poem. The contingency of the narrative events in the poem, juxtaposed with the expectation, partly created by Eliot's notes, of a symbolic order, exactly parallels the situation of being on a quest without knowledge of the goal of the quest. The random and fragmentary movement of the poem is never resolved; the poem's allusive conclusion is the most fragmented and dispersive passage of the poem. But the movement itself, the pull forward by a mythical goal, an ending, an explanation, is not rejected. Only the expectation of reaching that goal, an expectation which leads to despair, is rejected. This is why we can talk about structure at all in such a fragmented poem. The poem moves rhythmically among voices and among metaphoric and metonymic sections. And importantly, the barren, inhuman red rock episode occurs only in the first section of the poem and then, more extensively, in the final section as a state of exhaustion with and rejection of the constant movement of thwarted desire. In the final section, when the horrible consequences of stasis are most suggested, the poem opens itself most fully to a questing existence. Finitude must be accepted along with our attempts to protect ourselves from it: "These fragments I have shored against my ruins" (l. 431). The world arises from this interplay.

Metonymy, as the figure of relation, preserves the always already meaningfulness of the coherent world, as well as the limitless potential for new meaning, since relational meaning is not fixed meaning. In *The Waste Land* the narrative sections are important for more than thematic purposes. The metonymy grounds the poem by providing the common world in which we drink coffee, or make conversation, or come home from work. But the fragmentary nature of these narratives, caused by the metaphoric technique of the poem, emphasizes the contingency of this world and its resistance to symbolic enclosure. The parataxis and symbolism in the poem set in motion a restless search for meaning which can never be satisfied because of the metonymic density of the world, just as the metonymic realism sets up expectations for a coherent world which are shattered by the creative force of metaphoric intervention.

This combination of narrative and symbolism in *The Waste Land* poetically presents the absence of essence in the poem. This absence is more complete than a merely symbolic presentation of nothingness which fills the void with the *idea* of nothingness. In undercutting the idea, the poem releases absence as no-thing, but as a function of the dense and changing particularity of the world. The metonymic sections are not at all illustrations of ideas, even though some thematic threads can be traced through these sections. The details simply exceed the themes.

The example of this metonymy least complicated by the presence of allusion, which will be discussed later, is the presentation of character in "A Game of Chess." The voice of the hysterical woman and the voice of the woman in the pub are rendered naturalistically. On the manuscript Pound writes "photography" beside the lines of the hysterical woman, indicating that the conversation is *too* naturalistic.[11] Eliot's effort to capture the reality of these

11. *Facsimile* edition, 11–12.

characters goes far beyond the need to illustrate an idea or feeling about women or sex or relationships. Instead, Eliot is focusing on the object and finding the ideas and feelings there. In the pub scene, the woman's story is diverting, shapeless, full of asides, unfinished, pointless, and opaque to any meaning other than the presentation of the narrator's smug nosiness and Lil's weary plight. In presenting the world of these characters, Eliot lets it reveal its own metaphoric power. The repeated call of the bartender "HURRY UP PLEASE ITS TIME" is a metonymic detail which in the the context of *The Waste Land* (and especially in juxtaposition with the line evoking death: "Pressing lidless eyes and waiting for a knock upon the door") gains symbolic force through repetition until it undermines the solidity of the narrative world. Once this happens, the voice of the woman metamorphoses into Ophelia's voice:

> Ta Ta. Goonight. Goonight.
> Good night, ladies, good night, sweet ladies, good night,
>   good night. (ll. 171–73)

This metaphoric juxtaposition may remind us of Ophelia's song just preceding her good-byes, a song of a maiden ruined by a man's incontinence, just as Lil is ruined by Albert's attentions. But more important is the sudden broadening of the woman's voice to include Ophelia's voice, reminding us of the instability of self and its linguistic connection to a broader culture. The allusiveness of a language is all-inclusive.

IV

Allusion is a key to this poem, combining the metaphoric and metonymic function and inspiring the constant metamorphosis of style, structure, syntax, character, etc. This most outstanding figure of the poem has been the source of many quest-myth or thematic interpretations of the poem. But while the allusions have been thoroughly cataloged and classified, their function as a figure of speech remains somewhat of a mystery. I would not deny the thematic importance of the poem's allusions; but while they invariably enrich the poem emotionally and intellectually, thematic meaning is not dependent on the allusions, and recognition of allusions does not guarantee understanding of the poem. In other words, the main function of the allusions is not to provide an ironic comparison between past and present. The poem presents the eternal human condition of loss, mutability, and desire whether the allusions are recognized or not. For the reader without knowledge of the allusions, the poem has less density of meaning, but not a different meaning.

Even so, a general cultural awareness remains important for this poem. Eliot's notes insist that every reader confront the allusiveness of the poem and the cultural nature of linguistic material. The poem is not an expression of a sensibility but of a world. Eliot's allusions are usually to works that are culturally significant (rather than personally significant as many of Pound's tend to be) such as the Bible, Shakespeare, Dante, Virgil, Ovid, Spenser, St. Augustine, Milton, the quest myth, Buddha, the Upanishads. The majority of the allusions in *The Waste Land* are to texts which have been absorbed into the culture and have actually shaped our world. The allusions, like the metonymy, self-reflexively establish a common world which both fills our consciousness and yet extends far beyond it.

Allusion—from the Latin *alludere*, to play with—is preeminently a metonymic figure; the allusion is the part which stands for the whole text or situation it comes from. Yet its function is often described as metaphoric, since allusion brings two things into juxtaposition—its original context and its present context, creating a new, larger context. In combining metonymic and metaphoric functions, allusion does indeed show the play of language at its fullest and reveals the allusiveness of all language. A word has meaning only as part of a systemic whole; its meaning is in relation to its use in previous contexts. But each new use of a word adds a new context to its possibilities for meaning, changing that systemic whole. In this relation of part to whole, the whole is not complete or stable, but is defined by the part even as the part defines the whole in a hermeneutic relationship. The work's meaning is in the tension between its previous contextual definition and its present context.

In literary allusions a similar tension is always present. The relation of the text alluded to and the new text is never simply a comparison between two wholes. The work alluded to reflects upon the present context even as the present context absorbs and changes the allusion. This simple lesson of effective history, or of tradition in Eliot's theory, is regularly overlooked in *The Waste Land*, even though the allusions in the poem are so carefully woven into the fabric of the poem. The allusions are as much a part of the poem's world as the narratives and symbols; metonymically, the allusions establish a common cultural world dense with possibility, but metaphorically the allusion is transforming this world by the introduction of a new being.

For example, the line from *The Tempest*, "Those are pearls that were his eyes," appears in *The Waste Land* during the Madame Sosostris episode (l. 48) and the first conversation in "A Game of Chess" (l. 125); both episodes are largely metonymic in their naturalistic dialogue, but with portentous cosmic overtones. The chatty voice and the irrelevant details beginning and ending the Madame Sosostris section encompass the symbolic litany of the Tarot, nicely imaging how concrete and particular existence exceeds universal meaning. The line from Shakespeare, by virtue of its parenthetical enclosure and its tonal difference, seems to be a personal, "subjective" response to the conversation, differing from either the metonymic empirical feel of the narrative or the metaphoric import of the Tarot: "Here, said she, / Is your card, the drowned Phoenician Sailor, / (Those are pearls that were his eyes. Look!)" (ll. 46–48). The emotion in this line is clearly not the unique response of a self but is wholly contained by a cultural object. The emotional force in the line is partly due to its attention to its object—the perfection of Ariel's objective correlative. But this line is not simply a flashback to *The Tempest*. The evocation of personal mortality and the melancholy fascination with the image of the drowned man inhere in the line by virtue of the context of *The Waste*

Land in which the line is juxtaposed with the melancholy Tristan and Isolde episode, surrounded by the portentous prophecy of the Tarot (the drowned Phoenician Sailor is *your* card), and followed by the Dantesque vision of the living dead. When the line occurs in Ariel's song in *The Tempest*, the reader knows that no one has died in the storm—nor will anyone die—and while Ferdinand grieves over his father's wreck, his thoughts are so far from lingering on the death that he falls in love within thirty lines. In fact, Ariel's songs calm Ferdinand's fears, distracting him from melancholy. Only after reading *The Waste Land* is it impossible to hear Ariel's song as a mere ditty. In the diacritical system which is tradition, *The Waste Land* has changed *The Tempest* even while the magical vision of *The Tempest* contributes to the creation of *The Waste Land*.

The second occurrence of this line, in "A Game of Chess," is often interpreted by critics as showing the contrast between a sterile present and a rich past. At this point in the poem, the line refers to its previous occurrence in "The Burial of the Dead" as well as to *The Tempest*, thus reinforcing its modern accretion of meaning. The contrast in this passage between the voice of the woman and the voice of the narrator presents two different responses to the same situation, the same absence of purpose and self. The woman tries to fill the emptiness with a nervous flow of words demanding that *something* (not nothing) be said, thought, known, seen, remembered, that questions be answered, that uncertainties be clarified, and that plans be made. Her insistence on not speaking of the absence deprives her speech of possibility. Trapped in herself, she has nothing to say, no flexibility of idea or syntax. The narrator, on the other hand, focuses on the nothingness and finds a veritable treasure of ways of speaking (as the corpse reveals its treasure to Ariel's gaze), even though he finds no remedy for the initial situation.

> "What are you thinking of? What thinking? What?
> "I never know what you are thinking. Think."
>
> I think we are in rats' alley
> Where the dead men lost their bones.

                                                                    "Do
"You know nothing? Do you see nothing? Do you remem-
    ber
"Nothing?"

    I remember
Those are pearls that were his eyes.
"Are you alive, or not? Is there nothing in your head?"

                                                                    But

O O O O that Shakespeherian Rag—
It's so elegant
So intelligent (ll. 113–16 and 121–30)

Each of the three responses of the narrator in this passage provides
a greater element of play to counter the anxiety of self-doubt. The
fierce image of rats' alley confirms the hopelessness of their situation, but also the power of words to create the precise emotion which
the woman's repetitive emptiness sadly lacks. The allusion to *The
Tempest*, while still a meditation on death, affirms the narrator's
connection to the cultural world, and also expresses an understanding that death allows metamorphosis, even as the lack of self allows potent world and cultural forces to speak. Allusion is a transformation of world and creation of self. The final response, an
allusion to a popular song, is itself a transformation of Shakespeare
into a modern "Shakespeherian Rag." Ariel's song returns to an in-
consequential ditty, as the world flows into the void of the self. The
schmaltzy play of language in these three lines represents a healthy
release from the woman's isolated self-consciousness. The woman,
insisting upon answers, finds only emptiness. The narrator, ac-
cepting the absence of answers, finds a world, though not the world
of beauty and meaning he might desire. The world is diacritical and
linguistic, a play of possibilities. Allusion's combination of the
transforming power of metaphor and the cultural connectedness of
metonymy makes it a central figure of the hermeneutic world.

   Our cultural system determines how we see the world but also
allows for metamorphosis. The poem is not able to escape this
shifting world in theme, syntax, or structure. The sea-change of

Phlebas and the metamorphosis of Philomela only reinforce the non-essential nature of the things of the poem. The objects of the poem are alive and changing, losing definition and fixity under the pressure of allusion, metaphor, and metonymy. This metamorphosis of the world is the point of the poem; no other idea or feeling exceeds it. The poem's movement is toward an acceptance of this absence of essence, toward the understanding of the freedom which accompanies the anxiety of the hermeneutic world. This culmination will become clear in an examination of "What the Thunder Said," but first let me briefly clarify the psychic implications of these poetic elements of this poem.

V

In *The Waste Land* the presentation of absence is not fully explained by the conjunction of poetic technique and the existential state of man, since the poem seems obsessed by a very particular problem—the relationship with the other, particularly the sexual relationship. The sense of anxiety and loss in the poem is not related to modern technology as much as to psychic forces, though the psyche is, of course, part of being in a world. And considering the very real disturbance of Eliot's psyche in 1921, it is surprising that more critical attention has not been given to psychological mechanisms in the poem.

While *The Waste Land* cannot represent a consciousness, because of the diversity of voices, or a collective consciousness, because of the unique particularity of much of the poem, there are some fruitful comparisons to be made between the poem and the Freudian unconscious, especially as this unconscious has been interpreted by Jacques Lacan, who has applied Heideggerian principles to Freud. We must remember that, for Freud, the unconscious is not at all available to consciousness except in analysis of its effects. So while the unconscious is always a particular unconscious in a particular body, it is not what we generally think of as the self. The mechanisms of the unconscious are beyond our control; they are largely responsible for placing the self, as an independent and autonomous entity, in suspicion. Lacan first explicitly connected this unconscious to language, as the other which forms our self, even though Freud points the way toward this interpretation with his analysis of puns and words in dreams.

For Lacan, the unconscious is structured diacritically like a language, and linguistic material is a major part of the unconscious. These basic principles have led Lacan to two formulations which are especially helpful in studying *The Waste Land*. The first, in the words of Lacan's translator and commentator Anthony Wilden, is that "the subject is the binary opposition of presence and absence."[12] Thinking about the diacritical composition of language and about the genesis of numbers, Lacan asserts that you must have two before you can have one, because there can be no sense of identity before there is difference to define that identity. That is, it is meaningless to talk of the one, if there is only one. The relationship between the one and the two is circular, hermeneutic.[13] In language, as in numbers, the identity of a sign is only meaningful in relation to other signs; in itself it is nothing. Now, Lacan sees this same principle in operation in the human psyche. Initially, the infant has no self identity, nor any sense of the difference of the mother from itself. Only as the infant feels the absence of the mother is any notion of a self possible. But this sense of self is always defined by the absent other; the self is a lack of wholeness. For Lacan, the primordial and unsatisfiable desire of the subject is to recover this wholeness, even though the recovery of wholeness would have to mean the loss of the self which desires and is defined by the lack. I hope the reader will hear the echoes of Eliot's dissertation in this. Nonrelational, immediate experience is "annihilation and utter night" (KE, 31) for the subject, because the subject is only given at the same time as other selves are given. Loss of relations means loss

12. Jacques Lacan, *The Language of the Self: The Function of Language in Psychoanalysis*, trans. Anthony Wilden (New York, 1968), 191.
13. Jacques Lacan, "Of Structure as an Inmixing of Otherness Prerequisite to Any Subject Whatever," in Macksey and Donato (eds.), *The Structuralist Controversy*, 191.

of self (KE, 150). As we have seen, relations are linguistically given; Lacan's ideas become extremely difficult as he discusses the element of language in the formulation of the subject. Lacan has made famous Freud's observation of the child who repeatedly makes his toy disappear and reappear, saying *"fort . . . da"* ("gone . . . there"). Freud has several speculations about this game, but Lacan seizes on it as related to the creation of self and others in absence. In the game, the child is reenacting the separation from the mother, mastering it through the manipulation of symbols. In play, the child can control the absence and presence of the other. In this way the child is meaningfully placed in the diacritical system of language wherein the signification of *fort* and *da* depend upon each other and by which presence can be achieved from absence. The word, like the self, is defined by the absence of the other. The initial loss, the recognition that you are not whole or self-sufficient, is also the moment of immersion in the linguistic world.[14]

In the linguistic manipulation of presence and absence, the child is trying to fill the lack, but the lack is what permits his language. Wilden explains, "For the object to be discovered by the child it must be *absent.*" The way we try to make the other present to ourselves—through language—ensures that it will be absent. As Eliot never tires of emphasizing in his dissertation, relations, the ideal, are not the real, even though the ideal is the only real for us. This leads us to the second of Lacan's formulations which is of interest here. Because of the connection between language and desire for the other, Lacan is able to connect psychic and linguistic mechanisms. Thus, he analyzes the connection between the unconscious mechanisms of condensation and displacement and the linguistic categories of metaphor and metonymy. Lacan's main interest seems to be in displacement and metonymy, which constantly avoid the psychic problem by calling up something contiguous and irrelevant to the problem to displace it (unlike metaphor, where what is not said is clearly represented in the figure): "metonymy, by the displacement of the 'real' object of the subject's desire onto some-

---

14. Lacan, *Language of the Self*, 106–108, 159–67.

thing apparently insignificant, represents the *manque d'être* (lack of being) which is constituent of desire itself."[15] In other words, metonymy tries to avoid the absence even while it reveals the most primordial absence.

This brief and necessarily oversimplified sketch of Lacan will suffice for my present intentions. *The Waste Land* enacts a loss of the other which is also a discovery of the insufficiency of the self (fear of death) and the entry into the linguistic world. The poem has a wish to return to a nonrelational and static state, a wish brought on by the fear of death and time which results from the initial separation from the other. In the poem, the other is simultaneously spurned as a symbol of the insufficiency of the self and yearned for as completing and annihilating the self. But the only positive conclusion can be an acceptance of the absence of the other in the self.

The poem opens with a desire to return to stasis, to a living death of "dull roots," "dried tubers," and "forgetful snow" before the generation which creates "memory and desire." The anxiety about change, and also the already potent workings of desire, cause a metonymic displacement from the painful thought of change to an irrelevant story connected only by continuity between winter and summer. The movement into the Marie episode seems to continue this displacement, but a curious thing happens here. As in the Munich episode, the narrator is not alone in this memory. Marie's fears of the mountain are soothed by her companion, and the release of the ride down the mountain turns into a positive sense of freedom. But, I would argue, the freedom is not connected to the mountains so much as to the other and the desire expressed in the ride down the mountain. Her sentence veers away from the mountains and from herself: "In the mountains, there you feel free" (l. 17). The feeling is in the second person, the possibility of the other. But the recognition of this other is too painful. The memory—initially a harmless displacement—becomes the desire which is being avoided. The "you" shifts suddenly to "I" and memory is displaced by the safer limitation of the present tense: "I read, much of the

15. *Ibid.*, 163, 242. Again, these are Wilden's words.

night, and go south in the winter" (l. 18). In the memory of the other, the self is seen in its isolation. But if the self can confine itself to the present moment, out of time, then it can pretend that it is sufficient and does not need the anxiety or freedom brought on by the other. The solution to anxiety about death is an assertion of the isolated self over the power of desire.

The sterility of this situation of the isolated self metaphorically changes into the barren vision of the red rock passage. This vision is a reprise of the opening lines, but is harsher: the dull roots now "clutch," the dead land is now "stony rubbish," the shelter is no longer forgetful snow but the shadow of the red rock, and the "little life" is reduced to a "handful of dust." The inklings of April must not be allowed. But away from memory and desire, there is no world for the self. Because metonymy is the figure of desire which creates a world to fill the lack of wholeness, the total erasure of desire also erases the world—only the barren waste remains. The compulsive repetition in this section presents this state of regression to changelessness.

The transition from this bleak state to the lines in German from *Tristan and Isolde* is abrupt. The limited and repetitive diction and syntax of the red rock section are completely overwhelmed by the possibility of an entirely different language. And the evocation of the sea, the fresh breeze, and the desire for the other displaces the sterility of the isolated self.

> *Frisch weht der Wind*
> *Der Heimat zu*
> *Mein Irisch kind*
> *Wo weilest du* (ll. 31–34)

("The wind blows fresh to the homeland. My Irish girl, where are you lingering?"[16]) The rich possibilities carried by this new language result from the need to cover the lack of being revealed by the withdrawal into the self. The vision of death in the handful of dust

16. Translation from B. C. Southam, *A Guide to the Selected Poems of T. S. Eliot* (New York, 1968), 74.

is specifically countered by Eros. This expression of love and desire is not particular and painful; it is cultural, displaced from the self into an allusion to one of our culture's most famous tragic love stories. Here, allusion is a way to displace the anxiety about the lack revealed in desire, even though the allusion also points up the absence of the self which allows culture to speak. Like metonymy, allusion both fills in the absence of the self and emphasizes it.

Only within the confines of the cultural allusion is the particular expression of desire able to be expressed. The voice of the hyacinth girl calls up one of the most interesting and perplexing passages in the poem:

> —Yet when we came back, late, from the hyacinth garden
> Your arms full, and your hair wet, I could not
> Speak, and my eyes failed, I was neither
> Living nor dead, and I knew nothing,
> Looking into the heart of light, the silence.
> *Oed' und leer das Meer.* (ll. 37–42)

The seemingly incidental narrative about the hyacinth girl, developing metonymically from the presumably safe allusion to *Tristan and Isolde*, leads straight into the heart of the trauma. The self and world are annihilated in love and in a simultaneous loss of love. These lines suggest both the mystical ecstacy of union and an absolute bereftness, total loss of even the knowledge of what is lost. These lines present an unthinkable and unbearable union of love and loss, for absolute union with the other means loss of the self, as discovery of the self means a painful separation from the other. This enactment of the trauma of the child is the psychic center of the poem, imaging the cosmic bonding between death and desire.

The hyacinth girl episode ends wth another allusion to *Tristan and Isolde*, this time to the end of the opera as the dying Tristan yearns to see Isolde once more. In the allusion, the uncommunicable feeling of the preceding lines is brought to expression by being distanced from the self into a cultural object, just as, once again, the allusion Eliot has chosen realizes Tristan's feeling in an object, the waste and empty sea. This movement out away from the self is where freedom lies. Rather than trying to make do in the barrenness of the self because of the anxiety about desire and death, one must realize the possibilities given to us by this absence which allows the other to speak for us. The objective correlative becomes a psychological principle.

This principle functions in a similar way in the Unreal City episode in "The Burial of the Dead." Here, the empirical London of Madame Sosostris is raised to a symbolic London which escapes change in a vision of eternal Hell. The many allusions to Dante in this episode, along with the repetitive meter and assonance, universalize the passage in a way reminiscent of the opening lines of the poem. The metaphoric emphasis of the Unreal City in both poetic technique and in symbolic reference suggests finality and completion: "With a dead sound on the final stroke of nine" (l. 68). But the finality is challenged in the next line when a particular "I" and a human voice are introduced into this muffled and mechanized scene of universal damnation: "There I saw one I knew, and stopped him, crying: Stetson!" (l. 69). Like Dante's recognition of a face in the Inferno, this recognition of the other is both a relief from the inhuman scene and a horror of understanding your own culpability and your division from the other. That is, you recognize your own fault—spiritually in sin and psychologically incomplete. The other both saves from the inhuman and damns into division. "The Burial of the Dead" ends by drawing you, the reader, "hypocrite lecteur," into this conflict.

The texture of these last eight lines of section I is also very different from that of the preceding eight. The images here are surrealistic in a prickly, disturbing way, as opposed to the monotone depression beginning the episode, and the rhythm of the language is conversational and questioning—distinctly human. With the oddness of the images, the allusions to Baudelaire and Webster, and the dramatic address to the other, we are again led out of symbolic enclosure into the particular and opaque world of human culture where death and desire disturb our bed.

The sexual relationship is where the conjunction of death and desire is always most powerful and disturbing. The poem returns again and again to the imperfection of the sexual union, indeed to its deathlike quality, in the allusions to Cleopatra and Dido (at the beginning of "A Game of Chess") who comitted suicide for love, in the abortion of Lil, the rape of Philomela, the emptiness of the typist, the ruin of the Thames-daughters. Even the Virgin Queen has her Leicester, and Parsifal must conquer his lust. No human is exempt. These unbearable scenes are the stuff of the world, the inevitable impurity of a world where desire cannot be satisfied. Finitude is our original sin, not the result of it, so we are never free from the most basic fault—lack—which triggers our desires.

Many of these sexual references are clustered in "The Fire Sermon." But this section also introduces a new quality of voice which is not portentous, nor grieving, nor narrative in a neutral or satiric way. These new voices suggest a purity not yet debased. The repeated quotation from Spenser's "Spousal Song," "Sweet Thames, run softly, till I end my song" (ll. 176, 183), is in its original context a gentle and happy refrain celebrating ideal marriage. Even though, in the context of Eliot's poem, the line seems to stress the word "end," still, this allusion is unlike any preceding one of the poem in that it carries no explicit weight of loss, death, or dread. Also, the line from Verlaine, "*Et O ces voix d'enfants, chantant dans la coupole!*" (l. 202), is generally taken to represent the pure voices of children celebrating Parsifal's triumph, while the Rhine maidens' song, "Weialala leia/Wallala leialala" (ll. 277–78), occurs at the opening of the *Ring* cycle before the river's gold is stolen. These lines, along with the line "Inexplicable splendour of Ionian white and gold," speak of something miraculously beautiful. Here, in the structural center of the poem, lyrical song becomes a possibility for speaking. This possibility is hinted at in the lovely song from *Tristan and Isolde* which interrupts the first red rock episode, and yet the sadness of that song mitigates its beauty and leads to further despair. Now in "The Fire Sermon" the possibility returns that out of the rather sordid world of "A Game of Chess" speaking may metamorphose into the inviolable voice of the nightingale.

But no voice in a world is inviolable. The lilting line from Spenser gradually changes within its new context. In conjunction with an allusion to Psalm 137, the happy song begins to sound like weeping, and even the stable iambic pentameter generates an alexandrine:

> By the waters of Leman I sat down and wept . . .
> Sweet Thames, run softly till I end my song,
> Sweet Thames, run softly, for I speak not loud or long.
> (ll. 182–84)

Then the marriage song metonymically calls up Marvell's seduction song, where Time has become its more literal manifestation, Death:

> But at my back in a cold blast I hear
> The rattle of bones, and chuckle spread from ear to ear.
> (ll. 185–86)

The conjunction of sex and death is once again suggested as the allusion to Marvell undergoes one more mutation:

> But at my back from time to time I hear
> The sound of horns and motors, which shall bring
> Sweeney to Mrs. Porter in the spring. (ll. 196–98)

Eliot's note to these lines refers us to the story of Actaeon and Diana, in which sexual interest results in a horrible death. And the ballad about Mrs. Porter much debases the Spenserian song with which the section began, especially in the juxtaposition of the original text in which ideal love triumphs and the original off-color ballad in which Mrs. Porter and her daughter are washing something other than their feet.

Throughout "The Fire Sermon," the tantalizing glimpses of beauty offered in moments of song are, in our errancy, taken as something other than manifestations of the same desire, which, as sexual, reduces the song to a dirty joke. Philomela can sing as a nightingale because she has been violated; that her song, too, is violated into the leering "Jug jug" shows the constancy and complexity of the force of desire. Each type of singing depends on the possibility of the other, and singing comes to represent the unresolved state of being human.

The song of Mrs. Porter is interrupted, not by the pure voices of the children singing for Parsifal, but by a reference to these voices singing in the distance: *"Et O ces voix d'enfants, chantant dans la coupole!"* The distancing effects of this reference and the fluidity of French after the sing-song English ballad suggest another world entirely than the British world of Sweeney. (Even in Verlaine we hear this difference from Parsifal's world of lust and bloody battle.) This momentary vision is mocked by the prosaic "Twit twit twit" of the much reduced nightingale's song.

The music returns at the end of the typist section, starting with a "record on the gramophone" (l. 256), becoming Ariel's mysterious music in an allusion to *The Tempest*, " 'This music crept by me upon the waters' " (l. 257), and then the more empirical "Pleasant whining of a mandoline" (l. 261). Each of these references—to the empty world of the typist, the magic world of Ariel, and the neutral, everyday world—tells of a different way of singing. This remarkable recurrence of music out of misery is gathered up in the magnificent line, "Inexplicable splendour of Ionian white and gold." The reference to religion and the wonder of divine redemption beyond this world of singing is, of course, clear. But the anapestic music of the line is also powerful. "Ionian" suggests not only architecture, but also the Ionics of Greek metrics, and the quantitative principle of classical verse is surely at work in the rhythm of this line.

This expansive burst of song seems to grow out of the first emotionally neutral and world-accepting passage in the poem since the scene of drinking coffee in the Hofgarten. The communal Hofgarten is now replaced by a "public bar" where "fishmen" meet for lunch. The "pleasant" and everyday nature of this scene displaces the indifference and loneliness of the typist as a way of breaking out of depression. But perhaps under the influence of the vibrating word "fishmen" (a vision of mermans?), the vision in the church violates the metonymic regularity of this normal, communal world. So even while the vision offers great beauty, it does so at great expense. And with the next lines of the poem, we feel that the singing of the Thames daughters is stifled. These lines are the shortest in the poem, breaking up the flow of syntax and emphasizing metaphoric substitutions rather than metonymic connections. Indeed, the centering of these very short lines on the page makes the long, Ionian line appear to rest upon the following stanzas like a capital on its column, as if the symbolic thrust of "Inexplicable splendour" rests upon the certainty of fragmentation and loss of meaningful connections: "I can connect / Nothing with nothing" (ll. 301–302). The "white and gold" become "oil and tar" and the river song is once again of sexual degradation.

This is an unbearable state, and as a response to this paradox, the ending of "The Fire Sermon" is the greatest forgetting of errancy in the poem. The wish to be purged of desire is the vehement response to the sexuality which undermines the few fleeting glimpses of beauty. But you cannot cure the self by getting rid of desire, since the human is defined in its happiness and misery by that desire. The purging of desire and consequent loss of humanity are what lead us into the extended desert section opening "What the Thunder Said." But much of our agony may be spared if the self did not feel it had to fight the desire. We do not need to burn, but rather we need to disperse our selves into the fecund and music-giving water. "Death by Water" is an alternative to burning. The solution is not to erase the desire and keep the self—that gives us the barren waste. The solution is to erase the self and keep the desire.

VI

This understanding leads us into the resolution of the poem. The beginning of "What the Thunder Said" returns us to the technique and tonality of the red rock section in "The Burial of the Dead." The metaphoric/symbolic syntax and diction again distance us from a meaningful world, but now there is an explicit recognition of the failure of symbolic escape from death and desire, the failure of a savior to save from death:

> He who was living is now dead
> We who were living are now dying
> With a little patience. (ll. 328–30)

The desire for water to relieve the inhuman sterility of the wasteland is explicit, but there seems to be no way to create water from the prison of symbolic enclosure. The attempt to transform the symbols of barrenness is doomed to failure within the confines of the symbolic world. The language cannot blossom into a fertile world:

> If there were water
> And no rock
> If there were rock
> And also water
> And water
> A spring
> A pool among the rock
> If there were the sound of water only
> Not the cicada
> And dry grass singing
> But sound of water over a rock
> Where the hermit-thrush sings in the pine trees
> Drip drop drip drop drop drop drop
> But there is no water (ll. 346–59)

For a moment the hermit-thrush does sing in the pines. But the metaphoric fragmentation of language emphasizing the object— water—and ignoring the metonymic and syntactic relations which would complete the sentence indicates a failure of desire in its concealing/revealing function. The glimpse of the world brought forth with the hermit-thrush is fleeting and particular, concealing any vision of the whole. But the symbolic urge is to erase the fragmentary particularity and temporality in a whole. Thus, the categorical conclusion, "But there is no water." This imprisoned symbolic urge has forgotten errancy, forgotten that we can never escape the process of desire and memory which disallows essence and stability.

The rigid definition of the desert begins to dissolve under the re-emergence of desire, manifested in a blurring of clear and categorical distinctions which provokes the *questi*oning. Under stress, apparitions appear, denying the death of possibility, but offering only a haunted vision of the human world:

> —But who is that on the other side of you?
>
> What is that sound high in the air
> Murmur of maternal lamentation
> Who are these hooded hordes swarming
> What is the city over the mountains
> Cracks and reforms and bursts in the violet air
>
> (ll. 366–69, 372–73)

These visions have the quality of things glimpsed on the edge of vision, or illuminated in flash of lightning and then destroyed in darkness. They culminate in a passage unlike any other in the poem:

> A woman drew her long black hair out tight
> And fiddled whisper music on those strings
> And bats with baby faces in the violet light
> Whistled, and beat their wings
> And crawled head downward down a blackened wall
>
> (ll. 378–82)

These lines echo earlier images: the woman's hair in "A Game of Chess," the violet hour of "The Fire Sermon," the whisper of the sea in "Death by Water." With this series of surreal images, we are back in a realm of civilization and the other and out of the desert; it is a world of possibilities, though horrible possibilities. The mutations of the nightmare are a shock, existing on that twilight edge between the real and unreal. These surreal images show the particular taken up by a symbolic technique which does not respect metonymic relations. The surreal tries to create a fullness of meaning by manipulating symbols, even if the meaning is a nightmare vision. There is still an unwillingness to quit looking for symbolic wholeness.

But with that nightmare release we are brought to the traditional climax of the quest, the chapel perilous, where we find no peril. We have instead a return to the particular and the metonymic world, briefly attempted in the hermit-thrush vision. Again, the grass is singing and the bird sings. The chapel is empty, "only the wind's home. / It has no windows, and the door swings, / Dry bones can harm no one" (ll. 389–91). The portentous symbolism previously attached to the wind and the bones is now gone. Bones, like sagging doors, exist as the inevitable result of time. Death is finally accepted, but not as the peaceful descent of Phlebas. The cock crows "In a flash of lightning" (l. 394). This is a reawakening of desire, which now hears not the "dry sterile thunder" of the desert (l. 342) but a voice which must be understood: DA, a polysemic syllable which must be interpreted.

The extreme difficulty of these final lines of *The Waste Land*— of the interpretation of the thunder and the cultural fragments— lies in the deep paradox of our existence. We only learn to accept death, that absence at the center of our being, by attention to particulars which hold the mystery of time in their opaque being. But the particular only comes to its being through the metonymy of desire—desire which covers the absence and wishes to escape it. Therefore, the interpretation must lead into other interpretations, never dispelling the darkness, but always trying to dispell it. The thunder is interpreted as give, sympathize, and control—not explanations, but commands toward an activity of hermeneutic give and take. And each of these interpretations is further interpreted. In the Upanishads, the men interpret the meaning of DA as Give, the demons interpret the meaning as Sympathize, the gods interpret it as Control. What man gives is no-thing, but only "The awful daring of a moment's surrender" (l. 404), the gift of the other, of absence. The demons sympathize with our errancy; we are trapped in the prison of our desire for essence—yet at that violet hour, the mystery of the particular (here the enigmatic reference to "a broken Coriolanus") recurs, haunting us. The key confirms both the prison and the release; it is the absence or finitude which both traps us and gives us possibilities. The gods offer control, which brings exhilaration; our desire captures and is propelled by finite existence as the sails capture and are propelled by the wind. The only being is being-in-the-world.

Finally, "the arid plain" is no longer "my lands" (ll. 425–26); the "waste" and the "land" are sundered. But my land is not my self. The land is a world in which the other speaks, and this is a rich and full world speaking of childhood and adulthood, past and present, of myth, religion, art. The allusions speak where we could not speak, celebrating the absence which allows their joint existence. And yet, each fragment speaks of our ruin. London is crumbling. Arnaut Daniel must be purged of his lusts. Philomela wishes to flee her human degradation, and the Prince of Aquitaine is bereft in his abandoned tower. We are not to escape the ravages of time. But the satisfaction of the play will distract us from death—"Why then Ile fit you." Our true foundation is not death but is that ceaseless hermeneutic between desire and death in which finite existence always just escapes our efforts to capture it in the word.

Bibliography

Allan, Mowbray. *T. S. Eliot's Impersonal Theory of Poetry*. Lewisburg, Pa., 1974.

Ault, Donald. *Narrative Unbound: Re-visioning Blake's "Four Zoas."* Barrytown, N.Y., 1985.

Bachelard, Gaston. *On Poetic Imagination and Reverie: Selections from the Works of Gaston Bachelard*. Translated by Colette Gaudin. New York, 1971.

Bergonzi, Bernard. *T. S. Eliot*. New York, 1972.

Bolgan, Anne. *What the Thunder Really Said*. Montreal, 1973.

Bradley, F. H. *Appearance and Reality*. 2nd ed. Oxford, 1925.

————. *Essays on Truth and Reality*. Oxford, 1914.

Brooks, Cleanth. *"The Waste Land*: Critique of the Myth." *Modern Poetry and the Tradition*. Chapel Hill, 1939.

Culler, Jonathan. *Ferdinand de Saussure*. New York. 1972.

————. *Structuralist Poetics: Structuralism, Linguistics, and the Study of Literature*. Ithaca, 1975.

Derrida, Jacques. *Of Grammatology*. Translated by Gayatri Chakravorty Spivak. Baltimore, 1974.

————. "Differance." *Speech and Phenomena*. Translated by David B. Allison. Evanston, Ill., 1973.

————. "Structure, Sign, and Play in the Discourse of the Human Sciences." In *The Structuralist Controversy: The Languages of Criticism and the Sciences of Man*. Edited by Richard Macksey and Eugenio Donato. Baltimore, 1970.

————. "White Mythology." Translated by F. C. T. Moore. *New Literary History*, VI (1974), 5–74.

Drew, Elizabeth. *T. S. Eliot: The Design of His Poetry*. New York, 1949.

Durrell, Lawrence. *A Key to Modern Poetry*. London, 1952.

Eliot, T. S. *After Strange Gods*. New York, 1934.

————. *Collected Poems 1909–1962*. New York, 1963.

————. "Isolated Superiority." *Dial*, LXXXIV (1928), 4–7.

————. *Knowledge and Experience in the Philosophy of F. H. Bradley.* New York, 1964.

————. "London Letter." *Dial,* LXX (1921), 448–53.

————. *On Poetry and Poets.* New York, 1952.

————. *The Sacred Wood: Essays on Poetry and Criticism.* London, 1920.

————. *Selected Essays.* Rev. ed. New York, 1950.

————. *"The Waste Land": A Facsimile and Transcript of the Original Drafts Including the Annotations of Ezra Pound.* Edited by Valerie Eliot. New York, 1971.

Empson, William. *Seven Types of Ambiguity.* New York, 1947.

Foucault, Michel. *The Order of Things: An Archeology of the Human Sciences.* New York, 1973.

Frank, Joseph. "Spatial Form in Modern Literature." *Sewanee Review,* LIII (1945), 221–40, 433–56, 643–53.

Freed, Lewis. *T. S. Eliot: The Critic as Philosopher.* West Lafayette, Ind., 1979.

Frye, Northrop. *Fables of Identity: Studies in Poetic Mythology.* New York, 1963.

Gadamer, Hans-Georg. *Truth and Method.* New York, 1975.

Gardner, Helen. *The Art of T. S. Eliot.* London, 1949.

Heidegger, Martin. *Being and Time.* Translated by John Macquarrie and Edward Robinson. New York, 1962.

————. "On the Essence of Truth." In *Existence and Being.* Translated by R. F. C. Hull and Alan Crick. Chicago, 1949.

————. "The Origin of the Work of Art." In *Poetry, Language, Thought.* Translated by Albert Hofstadter. New York, 1971.

Hough, Graham. *Image and Experience.* London, 1960.

Kenner, Hugh. *The Invisible Poet: T. S. Eliot.* New York, 1959.

————. *The Pound Era.* Berkeley, 1971.

Kermode, Frank. "A Babylonish Dialect." *Sewanee Review,* LXXIV (1966), 225–38.

Korg, Jacob. "Modern Art Techniques in *The Waste Land.*" *Journal of Aesthetics and Art Criticism,* XVIII (1960), 456–63.

Lacan, Jacques. *The Language of the Self: The Function of Language in Psychoanalysis.* Translated by Anthony Wilden. New York, 1968.

————. "Of Structure as an Inmixing of Otherness Prerequisite to Any Subject Whatever." In *The Structuralist Controversy: The Language of Criticism and the Science of Man.* Edited by Richard Macksey and Eugenio Donato. Baltimore, 1970.

Laplanche, Jean, and Serge Leclaire. "L'Inconscient." *Les Temps Modernes,* XVII (July, 1961), 81–129.

Leavis, F. R. *New Bearings in English Poetry.* 1932; rpr. Ann Arbor, 1960.

Levi-Strauss, Claude. "The Structural Study of Myth." In *Structural Anthropology.* Translated by Claire Jacobson and Brooke Grundfest Schoepf. Garden City, N.Y., 1967.

Litz, A. Walton. "*The Waste Land* Fifty Years After." In *Eliot in His Time: Essays on the Occasion of the Fiftieth Anniversary of "The Waste Land."* Edited by A. Walton Litz. Princeton, 1973.

Mallarmé, Stéphane. *Selected Poems.* Translated by C. F. MacIntyre. Berkeley, 1965.

Margolis, John D. *T. S. Eliot's Intellectual Development, 1922–1939.* Chicago, 1972.

Martin, Jay, ed. *A Collection of Critical Essays on "The Waste Land."* Englewood Cliffs, N.J., 1968.

Miller, J. Hillis. *Poets of Reality.* New York, 1974.

Nevo, Ruth. "*The Waste Land*: Ur Text of Deconstruction." *New Literary History*, XIII (1982), 453–61.

Patterson, Gertrude. *T. S. Eliot: Poems in the Making.* Manchester, 1971.

Ransom, John Crowe. *The New Criticism.* New York, 1941.

———. *The World's Body.* New York, 1938.

Rasmussen, David M. *Mythic-Symbolic Language and Philosophical Anthropology: A Constructive Interpretation of the Thought of Paul Ricoeur.* The Hague, 1971.

Richards, I. A. *The Philosophy of Rhetoric.* 1936; rpr. New York, 1965.

———. *Principles of Literary Criticism.* 1924; rpr. London, 1930.

Richardson, William J. *Heidegger: Through Phenomenology to Thought.* The Hague, 1963.

Ricoeur, Paul. *Freud and Philosophy: An Essay on Interpretation.* Translated by Denis Savage. New Haven, 1970.

———. *Interpretation Theory: Discourse and the Surplus of Meaning.* Fort Worth, 1976.

———. "Narrative Time." *Critical Inquiry*, VII (Autumn, 1980), 169–90.

———. *The Rule of Metaphor: Multi-disciplinary Studies of the Creation of Meaning in Language.* Translated by Robert Czerny with Kathleen McLaughlin and John Costello. Toronto, 1977.

———. *The Symbolism of Evil.* Translated by Emerson Buchanan. Boston, 1969.

Saussure, Ferdinand de. *Course in General Linguistics.* Translated by Wade Baskin. Edited by Charles Bally and Albert Sechehaye. New York, 1959.

Smidt, Kristian. *Poetry and Belief.* 1949; rpr. London, 1961.

Smith, Grover. *T. S. Eliot's Poetry and Plays: A Study in Sources and Meaning.* Chicago, 1956.

Southam, B. C. *A Guide to the Selected Poems of T. S. Eliot.* New York, 1968.

Spanos, William. "Repetition in *The Waste Land*: A Phenomenological De-struction." *Boundary 2*, VII (Spring, 1979), 225–85.

Spender, Stephen. *T. S. Eliot.* New York, 1975.

Steiner, George. *Martin Heidegger.* New York, 1978.

Symons, Arthur. *The Symbolist Movement in Literature*. London, 1908.

Thormählen, Marianne. *"The Waste Land": A Fragmentary Wholeness*. Lund, 1978.

Tomlinson, Charles. *Poetry and Metamorphosis*. New York, 1983.

Turbayne, Colin M. *The Myth of Metaphor*. New Haven, 1962.

Weston, Jessie. *From Ritual to Romance*. 1920; rpr. Garden City, N.Y., 1957.

Wheelwright, Philip. *The Burning Fountain*. Bloomington, Ind., 1968.

Williams, William Carlos. *Selected Letters*. Edited by John C. Thirlwall. New York, 1957.

Williamson, George. *A Reader's Guide to T. S. Eliot*. New York, 1953.

Wilson, Edmund. *Axel's Castle*. New York, 1931.

Wimsatt, William K., and Cleanth Brooks. *Literary Criticism: A Short History*. New York, 1957.

Wollheim, Richard. "Eliot and Bradley: An account." In *Eliot in Perspective: A Symposium*. Edited by Graham Martin. London, 1970.

———. *F. H. Bradley*. Baltimore, 1969.

Index